Making Social Knowledge in the Victorian City

This study explores the 'ecology of knowledge' of urban Britain in the Victorian period and seeks to examine the way in which Victorians comprehended the nature of their urban society, through an exploration of the history of Victorian Manchester, and two specific case studies on the fiction of Elizabeth Gaskell and the campaigns for educational extension which emerged out of the city. It argues that crucial to the Victorians' approaches was the 'visiting mode' as a particular discursive formation, including its institutional foundations, its characteristic modes and assumptions, and the texts which exemplify it. Recognition of the importance of the visiting mode, it is argued, offers a fundamental challenge to established Foucauldian interpretations of nineteenth-century society and culture and provides an important corrective to recent scholarship of nineteenth-century technologies of knowing.

Martin Hewitt is Professor of History at Anglia Ruskin University, Cambridge, UK.

Making Social Knowledge in the Victorian City

The Visiting Mode in Manchester, 1832–1914

Martin Hewitt

 Routledge
Taylor & Francis Group

LONDON AND NEW YORK

First published 2020 by Routledge

2 Park Square, Milton Park, Abingdon, Oxon, OX14 4RN

605 Third Avenue, New York, NY 10017

Routledge is an imprint of the Taylor & Francis Group, an informa business

First issued in paperback 2020

British Library Cataloguing-in-Publication Data
A catalogue record for this book is available from the British Library

Library of Congress Cataloging-in-Publication Data
Names: Hewitt, Martin, 1962- author.
Title: Making Social Knowledge in the Victorian City: The Visiting Mode in Manchester, 1832-1914 / Martin Hewitt.
Description: London; New York, NY: Routledge/Taylor & Francis Group, 2020. | Includes bibliographical references and index. | Summary: "This study explores the 'ecology of knowledge' of urban Britain in the Victorian period and seeks to examine the way in which Victorians comprehended the nature of their urban society, through an exploration of the history of Victorian Manchester, and two specific case studies on the fiction of Elizabeth Gaskell and the campaigns for educational extension which emerged out of the city. It argues that crucial to the Victorians' approaches was the 'visiting mode' as particular discursive formation, including its institutional foundations, its characteristic modes and assumptions, and the texts which exemplify it. Recognition of the importance of the visiting mode, it is argued, offers a fundamental challenge to established Foucauldian interpretations of nineteenth century society and culture, and provides an important corrective to recent scholarship of nineteenth century technologies of knowing"– Provided by publisher.
Identifiers: LCCN 2019018711 | ISBN 9780367135683 (hardback) | ISBN 9780367135690 (ebook) | ISBN 9781000012217 (ePub) | ISBN 9781000005394 (Adobe) | ISBN 9781000018738 (mobi)
Subjects: LCSH: Gaskell, Elizabeth Cleghorn, 1810-1865–Criticism and interpretation. | Social learning–England–Manchester–History. | City and town life–England–Manchester–History. | Sociology–Methodology–History. | Manchester (England)–Social life and customs–19th century. | Manchester (England)–Social life and customs–20th century. | Manchester (England)–Intellectual life. | Manchester (England)–In literature. | Great Britain–History–Victoria, 1837-1901.
Classification: LCC HN398.M27 H483 2020 | DDC 303.3/2094273–dc23
LC record available at https://lccn.loc.gov/2019018711

ISBN: 978-0-367-13568-3 (hbk)
ISBN: 978-0-367-78793-6 (pbk)

Typeset in Times
by Deanta Global Publishing Services, Chennai, India

Contents

Figures

Abbreviations

BMJ	*British Medical Journal*
DPS	District Provident Society
EAS	Education Aid Society
FSS	*Elizabeth Gaskell. Four Short Stories*, introduced by Anna Walters (1993)
M&SSA	Manchester and Salford Sanitary Association
MB	*Mary Barton* (Penguin, ed. Stephen Gill)
MC	*Manchester Courier*
MCCP	Manchester City Council, *Proceedings*
MCM	Manchester and Salford City Mission
MCMAR	*Manchester City Mission Annual Report*
MCMMag	*Manchester City Mission Magazine*
MCN	*Manchester City News*
MG	*Manchester Guardian*
MOH	Medical Officer of Health
MSp	*Manchester Spectator*
MSS	Manchester Statistical Society
MTPAR	Ministry to the Poor, *Annual Report*
MWT	*Manchester Weekly Times*
MX	*Manchester Examiner and Times*
N&S	*North and South* (Penguin, ed. Martin Dodsworth)
NA	National Archives, Kew
NPSA	National Public Schools Association
SBV	School board officer
TMSS	*Transactions of the Manchester Statistical Society*

Acknowledgements

This work has been an undesirably long time in the making, originating in a paper presented to a conference organised in memory of David Englander on 'The History of Social Investigation' in 2005, and before that in work on visiting organisations in Manchester in the 1990s. As such, its debts are extensive and in many cases no doubt unconscious. I am particularly grateful to Rosemary O'Day who organised the 2005 conference, and to the participants in that conference, most especially Eileen Yeo, both for the extraordinarily stimulating nature of the papers and discussions and for the subsequent advice and encouragement. The work here has also gained much from the critical input of Donna Loftus, Pamela K. Gilbert, Barry Doyle, Simon Gunn and former colleagues at what is now Leeds Trinity University, and at the Universities of Manchester and Huddersfield. I'm particularly grateful for the support and encouragement of Tom Crook, whose own work, and in particular his excellent study *Governing Systems*, has done much to inform and contextualise the final form in which this work has emerged. Special mention also to Joanne Shattock and Lizzie Ludlow for providing comment and reassurance at very short notice on the chapter on Gaskell's fiction and to Charlotte Elcock for help in reproducing Brewer's *Bird's Eye View of Manchester*. Above all, though, this volume is dedicated to the staff of the local studies and archives department of the Manchester Central Library, in its various organisational guises over the past 35 years, and in particular to David Taylor and Richard Bond. Without their knowledge, help and encouragement, this work would not have been possible.

1 Introduction

The 'statistical moment' and its limits

Introduction

The focus of this study is what Eileen Yeo has termed the 'larger ecology of knowledge' of urban Britain in the Victorian period.[1] It seeks to examine the way in which Victorians comprehended the nature of the urban society in which they increasingly resided, by examining the interrelationship of a particular discursive formation, its institutional foundations, its characteristic modes and assumptions, and the texts which exemplify it.[2] Such a project operates at the intersection of a number of relatively discrete literatures, including the histories of sociology, statistics and social policy, the study of nineteenth-century liberalism (not least its implication in technologies of surveillance and governmentality), Victorian urban history, cultural geography and literary studies.

Manchester has loomed large in almost all of these literatures. As the 'shock city' of the age, it has been prominent as the focus of much of the writing which first sought to make sense of the new urban-industrial society.[3] The social and especially the sanitary conditions of Manchester have frequently been taken as paradigmatic.[4] In statistics, although the more recent works of Desrosieres, Schweber and Levitan have adopted a metropolitan focus, Manchester remains unchallenged as both locus and primary exemplar of the provincial statistical movement of the early Victorian period.[5] Above all, especially in Mary Poovey's *Making a Social Body* (1995), Patrick Joyce's *The Rule of Freedom* (2003) and Chris Otter's *Victorian Eye* (2008), Manchester has played a central role in sustaining an influential Foucauldian interpretation of Victorian literature and culture, which dominated scholarly interpretations of the Victorian period in the final decades of the twentieth century, and continues in many respects to be hegemonic especially in approaches to social knowledge.[6]

Collectively and in its component parts, this is a sophisticated literature which carefully incorporates a sense of subordinate and residual positions, and summary inevitable produces a rather crude version. Nevertheless, it can be said to have advanced a number of central propositions. That the statistical movement of the 1830s was part of the emergence in that decade and the 1840s of a number of institutions and practices of surveillance, including the mapping of the city and the development of new 'statistical' approaches which 'solved the problems of the invisibility of the poor'. That the penetration of the city by various forms of disciplinary observation facilitated the transfer of the authority of traditional groups such as clergymen and philanthropists to new groups of disinterested experts. That the decay of the local impetus to sociological inquiry around mid-century allowed expertise to become predominantly located in the developing agencies of the central state. That fundamental to the ideological work of these institutions and practices was the rendering of the working classes as passive and inert ('drained of agency and massified' as Pamela Gilbert puts it), and hence amenable to abstraction and classification.[7] That the results were, in Mary Poovey's phrases, 'the banishment of time' and the rendering of 'a Euclidian view of space as empty and amenable to mathematical calculation', legible and rational.[8]

While this literature has continued to exert a powerful hold on scholarly approaches to the nineteenth century, there have been challenges to a number of its defining positions.[9] Poovey herself has explored the contestation of the idea of the value-free fact as collected by statisticians.[10] Within the history of health in particular, a number of studies, and in particular Tom Crook's impressive *Governing Systems* (2016), have demonstrated the complex and contingent histories of the extension of systems of surveillance and intervention.[11] Several important studies of the history of nineteenth-century statistics have unpacked what Oz Frankel describes as the 'uneven and inconclusive' extensions of statistical regimes.[12] Led by Lauren Goodlad's manifesto 'Beyond the Panopticon' (2003), a number of recent studies of nineteenth-century realist fiction have sought to move beyond the abstracting imperatives which preoccupied earlier work to consider the ways in which literature complicated and often questioned the effacement of the individual in the aggregate.[13] All this work has challenged the 'hard' version of earlier Focauldianism. But it has tended to do so by a reworking of the tensions implicit in Foucault's own thought, often via a greater employment of Foucault's subsequent discussions of 'governmentality' and especially most recently of 'biopolitics'.[14] The focus remains the state and the development of its systems of surveillance and control, which are still assumed to be at the heart of approaches to modernisation and liberalism. Processes of oversight and control are being complicated but not decentred; although not absolutely effective for the individual, they are conceived as operating at the level of the 'population'; they arrive more slowly, but they are still the dominant structural device. They are less totalising, but in their emphasis on the normal and tolerance of deviation at the extremes, even more implicitly statistical.[15] Ultimately, we get much the same analysis of how technologies of knowledge, as Newsom-Kerr puts it, rendered urban populations 'calculable and viewable'.[16]

The argument advanced here seeks to go further than these recent challenges to offer a more fundamental rebuttal, by arguing not merely that Foucauldian impulses were less effective and more slowly implemented than was often implied, but that these impulses were not the primary mode of social knowledge formation, at least in respect of urban society as a whole, for the vast bulk of the Victorian period. It rejects suggestions that the impetus of the early Victorian statistical movement dried up in the face of diversion into other campaigns or under the impact of generational shifts, arguing that the discontinuity around mid-century in the history of statistics and social investigation was much less marked than has often been suggested (both in respect of the crisis of the 1840s and the novelty of Booth). The early Victorian years did indeed see new anxieties about, and approaches to, the creation of social knowledge, but although the works of Poovey and others vividly illuminate many of their dynamics, they dramatically overstate their distinctiveness from alternative approaches as well as their success. The problem of the invisibility of the poor was not solved in these years, traditional authority was not transferred from philanthropist and clergyman to disinterested servant of the state, or from amateur to expert. The working classes were not massified or rendered inert, not least because the new regimes of surveillance far from effacing time and space achieved the exact opposite.

Fundamental to any understanding of how this took place and why its effects were so enduring requires recognition of the centrality of what we can describe as the 'visiting mode' to the production and reproduction of social knowledge from the 1830s to the 1890s. What marked, I would suggest, the ecology of social knowledge in Victorian Manchester fostered by this 'visiting mode' was a process of double enplotment, in which the tracing of spatial patterns is bound up in the incorporation of narrative patterns; a 'simultaneous operation of time and space' to paraphrase the historical geographer David Harvey, which placed space and the patterns of human agency it inscribed at the heart of understandings of urban society.[17]

There is, of course, a significant kernel of truth in the Foucauldian analysis of early Victorian developments. It is hard to dispute that a new model of knowledge formation and a new epistemological regime emerged around Kay-Shuttleworth and the Manchester Statistical Society (MSS) in the 1830s, in which the conclusions of an emerging cadre of experts, quantified and tabulated, were to supersede individual experience and the impressions of inexpert observers. Commentators like the pro-manufacturing journalist William Cooke Taylor made explicit the intent to challenge alternative apparently more impressionistic approaches, contrasting the 'incontrovertible facts, the tables of mortality, the records of hospitals and police-offices, the registers of parishes and courts of justice', with 'figures of speech' or 'Pathetic tales, more than sufficient to supply a whole generation of novelists' which, he argued, were driving the pressure for factory legislation in the 1830s.[18] Likewise, developments in the state during the 1830s and 1840s, civil registration, the census, the reform of the Poor Law system, the new police forces, did encourage the sort of isotropism discussed by Poovey and Joyce: residents and visitors alike produced accounts of Manchester which involved descriptions of cleavage, social and spatial, which flattened all sense of difference within classes and districts, in which, as the French observer Leon Faucher put it, 'All the houses, all the streets, resemble each other'.[19]

At the same time, this picture, as Poovey herself admits, must be complicated; chronologically, psephologically, conceptually, methodologically and ultimately spatially.

In the first place, the early Victorian statistical moment as embodied by the Manchester Statistical Society was remarkably short-lived, driven by a particular conjunction of crisis and visibility in industrial society. The analysis of the social statisticians of the 1830s was primarily a *factory* analysis, its abstraction facilitated by an overriding focus on industrial relations in which an economic categorisation of individuals was extrapolated into a wider social description, and spatial issues were marginal. In works like Andrew Ure's *Philosophy of Manufactures* (1835), Manchester was presented as the archetype of a form of industrial production, and its social structure reduced to economic functions.[20] However, the initial preoccupation with 'factory society' was overturned in the later 1830s and early 1840s by the rapid shift in focus to sanitary questions and hence to broader urban conditions.[21]

In fact, the MSS was narrowly sectional, both politically, a legacy of its initial alignment with the city's early Victorian radical-Unitarian elite, and religiously. The political affiliations of over 90% of the Manchester-based paper presenters from 1853 to 1901 have been determined as Liberal,[22] and there was a similar if not quite so strong bias towards Nonconformity.[23] This sectionalism was also social and functional: although a number of its early activists were substantial manufacturers, from the 1850s onwards, the Statistical Society was dominated by the professional and service classes and by those involved more in campaigning activities in public health, education and social reform rather than active philanthropists and voluntary workers, or even city councillors. Indeed, the fragility of the statistical movement's influence and the unlikelihood of its having effected a decisive break either in modes of investigation or of understanding is reinforced by its rapid loss of vigour around 1840.[24] During the 1840s, the Statistical Society came close on a number of occasions to collapse, before reviving in the early 1850s. Its survival owed partly to the persistence of a small cadre of enthusiasts, most particularly John Roberton, local doctor and correspondent of Richard Cobden, but perhaps more fundamentally to its continued ability to serve as a forum for the discussion of a range of topics and issues including social and economic problems. Although the Statistical Society maintained a sense of its function as (as an 1886 editorial put it) 'an agency for the acquisition of information concerning the social condition of the people',[25] and was occasionally drawn into the sort of surveying work it had pioneered in the 1830s, from the 1840s the taproot of this activity was elsewhere. It was not so much that the supporters of the Statistical Society were distracted by other campaigns (although the intense local political rivalries generated by the campaign for incorporation and conflict over the Corn Laws inevitably diverted some of the energies of its supporters into other channels).[26] It was certainly not that the work of the social survey was taken over by government.[27] Rather, it was that the statistical movement's success in calling attention to Manchester's 'social ills' encouraged the coalescence of a number of more overtly campaigning associations whose single-issue focus was better suited to exerting pressure for action, identifying problems and sustaining the social investigative machinery which had proved beyond the resources of the Statistical Society.[28] As Theodore Porter has suggested, it was the interested, rather than the disinterested, expert who came to predominate.[29]

Sanitary reform provides one case in point. In the 1840s, spurred on by the parliamentary investigations of the early Victorian period, and furnished with a rich supply of data from the civil registration of births and deaths, Manchester's sanitary reformers presented the fruits of their professional experience and observation in a variety of forms and arenas.[30] A second outbreak of cholera in Manchester in 1849, and the establishment of the Board of Health by the 1848 Public Health Act, brought a further raft of local investigations and surveys, including John Leigh and Ner Gardiner *History of the Cholera in Manchester in 1849* (1850), and a series of very detailed reports on the townships of Manchester and Salford by the Board of Health's investigators.[31] This prompted the formation in 1853 of the Manchester and Salford Sanitary Association (M&SSA) which made considerable efforts to investigate the social conditions of the city, a role which was only partly superseded by the reports of the city's Medical Officers of Health (MOHs) after their appointment in 1868.[32] In like manner, the Statistical Society's sustained concern with the deficiencies of educational provision was transmitted to a number of local associations, including the District Provident Society (DPS) and the Manchester City Mission, culminating by the late 1840s in the Lancashire (subsequently National) Public Schools Association and the Manchester and Salford Education Bill Committee, as well as to the local temperance movement, many of which were driven forward or actively supported by a cadre of medics and social reformers closely tied to the Statistical Society group.[33] What is significant about all these movements is the extent to which their political operations were characterised by sustained efforts to uncover the precise details of the social conditions they sought to reform.

We need to treat sceptically the more hyperbolic claims of the social statisticians of the 1830s as to the conceptual or methodological transformation they had effected. It was not just that the statistical methods adopted were remarkably rudimentary, even by contemporary European standards.[34] It is scarcely too harsh to suggest that Statistical Society sociology in the 1830s did not progress beyond counting. And where discrete phenomena were hard to isolate, little effort was made to develop rigorous classificatory regimes. The early inquiries of the MSS, for example, relied on distinctions of domestic conditions which its principal agent conceded 'must always be … vague and varying' without 'any precise definition', and were in essence merely the result of subjective categorisation.[35] Even at this rudimentary level, the failure of many potential data sources forced recourse to claims based on experience rather than specific observation, claims which were easily replicable by the very groups the statisticians apparently sought to eclipse.[36] Although he professed to have 'avoided alluding to evidence which is founded upon general opinion, or depends merely upon matters of perception; and to have chiefly availed [himself] of such as admitted of statistical classification', this is a feature even of James Kay-Shuttleworth's foundational 1832 pamphlet, *The Moral and Physical Condition of the Working Classes in Manchester*, which at one point confessed that the statistics for houses wanting whitewashing 'fail[ed] to indicate their gross neglect of order, and absolute filth … much less can we obtain satisfactory statistical results concerning the want of furniture, especially of bedding, and of food, clothing and fuel'.[37] M&SSA activists like Ransome and Royston remained suspicious (and even dismissive) of statistics, preferring careful on-the-ground enquiries.[38] Kathrin Levitan has noted how anxieties about the extent to which aggregated statistics occluded people as individuals ensured that nearly all early-Victorian social analysis combined aggregation and individualisation.[39] For every Foucauldian moment in the 1830s and 1840s, it is possible to present a counterweight; as in the case of

Henry Gaulter's 1833 study of the 1832 Manchester cholera outbreak, with its constant intimation that his tables were only a crude agglomeration of individual examples whose specificity was crucial to their significance, or Thomas Dorrington's 1844 warning that 'mere figures in connection to so large a town as Manchester, can give a very slight and inadequate notion of the subject to which they refer, so many circumstances have to be taken into consideration that modify any statistical deductions that may thence be drawn'.[40]

Part of the difficulty was the limited scope and questionable accuracy of the statistical information that was being generated by the developing instruments of the state. Almost the first activity of the MSS had been a strident criticism of the findings of the 1833 Factory Commission, and this was followed by even more scathing criticism of the statistics presented to Parliament in the 1833 school returns, noting in the township of Manchester alone that 1 infant, 10 Sundays and as many as 176 day schools had been overlooked, with a combined roll of over 10,000 scholars.[41] These anxieties long endured. They were a persistent feature of discussions over education throughout the period, and they were particularly fundamental to discussions of public health, both because of the failure to extend the collection of data to the notification of communicable diseases, and because of the distortions inherent in key returns such as local mortality rates, which were marred by problems such as the deaths of paupers in extramural workhouses. As the Manchester health campaigner Aldoph Samelson commented as late as the 1880s, 'the Manchester death-rate is a quicksand, a snare, a lullaby, a passport to a fool's paradise'.[42]

A text such as Joseph Adshead's *Distress in Manchester* (1842), though at first glance following the pattern of the Statistical Society surveys, with its search for the 'exact truth' and its attempt to 'trust to the effect upon [the reader's] judgement of a few simple statements',[43] vividly illustrates the limited purchase of Poovey's version of statistical thinking. Adshead based much of his argument not on his tabulations (which relate primarily to basic demographic data) but on a discursive account, situated precisely in the urban topography. These often comprised direct quotations from the reports of the Manchester town missionaries, on whom Adshead relied heavily for his information, and 'than whom', he conceded, 'no persons are better qualified to speak of the condition of the labouring classes of this populous neighbourhood'.[44]

Reliance of this sort alerts us to the fact that the statisticians never succeeded in overthrowing the authority of the interested and impressionistic engagements of clerics, district visitors and town missionaries. There is little evidence that they ever tried. The initial membership of the Manchester Statistical Society was largely identical to that of the District Provident

Society, which was itself organised around the creation of a city-wide system of voluntary house-to-house visitation.[45] Perhaps the parliamentary inquiries of the 1840s tended to avoid clerical or missionary evidence in favour of medics or the functionaries of the new Poor Law or registration systems. But this was temporary. In truth, although the reforms of the 1830s and 1840s brought into existence new sources of social data and new types of officials, changes in personnel or documentation were limited. Despite the proliferation of offices, there was no real increase in manpower, rather a tendency to pluralism: Ner Gardiner, the clerk to the Manchester Guardians, was also the city's superintendent registrar; Manchester's district registrars were all medical men with existing expertise drawn from the very charitable institutions that the new configurations were apparently to supersede. A figure like Daniel Noble, a medical man who came to prominence in the 1830s as president of the Manchester Phrenological Society and an active member of the Literary and Philosophical Society, before taking a leading role in the 1840s in the sanitary movement, but who was also during the 1840s and early 1850s one of the medical officers of the Manchester Poor Law Union, might offer an example of the creation of new expertise, but such instances are rare.[46]

There was no extensive new cadre of disinterested experts. James Riddell Wood, the Statistical Society's principal agent in the 1830s, might have acquired some authority from the society's range of investigations, but he possessed little 'professional capital'; citations of the work of agents persistently demonstrated the need to explicitly buttress their authority as 'intelligent', 'paid' (and therefore presumably conscientious).[47] Even then, as Crook has pointed out, the 1838 report of the Manchester Statistical Society noted that the evidence of the paid agent had been double-checked against the personal knowledge of different gentlemen.[48] There was a gradual increase in municipal expertise, but the rate of increase was slow, capacity remained limited and municipal action often required energetic pressure from voluntary associations. In the same way, as new instruments of municipal inspection developed, they did so in close collaboration with existing visitors. The Bristol MOH in 1871 urged sanitary inspectors to 'be on terms of intimate friendship with the Scripture-reader and city missionary, most valuable source of information [sic]'.[49] Peter Gaskell's *Artisans and Machinery* (1836) repeatedly relied on the testimony of John Ashworth, the Minister to the Poor, and of the visitors of the District Provident Society, as did the investigations of other members of the Statistical Society circle, including Thomas Potter and Adshead.[50] Even in the 1840s there was no meaningful separation from clerics.[51] While Poovey is not unaware of the significance of the early visiting ideas of Thomas Chalmers, the London City Mission and the Bible Mission women, her account does not emphasise sufficiently the symbiosis of the statistical movement and the rapidly expanding visiting infrastructure. It was a question not just of personnel, but also of methodology. Dependence on visitors implied reliance on visiting as the primary technology of investigation and information gathering. The statistical moment itself probably originated with the 1832 Special Board of Health, which used unpaid inspectors to make house-to-house visits across the Manchester police districts. The first substantial MSS investigation operated street to street, although it focused on collecting information about schools rather than individual residences.[52] Indeed, visiting was the primary investigative technique employed by the Statistical Society in its enquiries of the 1830s. Its early reports on the provision of education demonstrated a commitment to local surveys based on house-to-house visitation, initially employed in the Miles Platting district of Manchester, reported to the British Association in 1834, and then extended to a number of surrounding towns which formed the basis of further reports to the British Association in 1837 and 1841.[53] A survey of the educational state of Pendleton, based on house-to-house visiting, was published in the *Journal of the London Statistical Society* in 1839. Visitation by medical officers was the central strategy developed to confront the cholera epidemics of 1832 and 1849.[54] Other 'experts' who participated in the statistical movement derived their knowledge and authority largely from variants on visiting, such as the Poor Law relieving officer with 'the poor under my visiting charge',[55] or medical men like Richard Baron Howard and John Leigh drawing on their extensive experience of house visits to working-class patients.[56]

Notes

1 Eileen Yeo, *The Contest for Social Science. Relations and Representations of Gender and Class* (1996), xv.

2 Of the sort explored by Ian Hacking, 'Statistical Language, Statistical Truth and Statistical Reasoning', in E. McMullin, *The Social Dimension of Science* (1992), and in the concept of 'phenomenotechnics' developed by T. Osborne and N. Rose, 'Spatial Phenomenotechnics: Making Space with Charles Booth and Patrick Geddes', *Environment and Planning D: Society and Space* 22 (2004), 209–28.

3 Including Asa Briggs, 'Manchester' in his *Victorian Cities* (1964); S. Marcus, *Engels, Manchester and the Working Class* (1974), Gary S. Messinger, *Manchester in the Victorian Age. The Half-Known City* (1985), Andrew Lees, *Cities Perceived. Urban Society in European and American Thought, 1820–1940* (1985).

4 Harold L. Platt's *Shock Cities: The Environmental Transformation and Reform of Manchester and Chicago* (2005), Stephen Mosley's *The Chimney of the World: A History of Smoke Pollution in Victorian and Edwardian Manchester* (2008) and Harriet Ritvo's *The Dawn of Green: Manchester, Thirlmere and Modern*

Environmentalism (2009) are the latest in a long line of texts using Manchester to explore the evolution of sanitary and environmental policy. Including John D. Wirth and Robert L. Jones, eds, *Manchester and Sao Paulo. Problems of Rapid Urban Growth* (1978).

5 Alain Desrosieres, *The Politics of Large Numbers. A History of Statistical Reasoning* (1998), L. Schweber, *Disciplining Statistics: Demography and Vital Statistics in France and England, 1830–1885* (2006) and also Tom Crook and Glen O'Hara, eds, *Statistics and the Public Sphere: Numbers and the People in Modern Britain, 1800–2000* (2011). For the older tradition, see T.S. Ashton, *Economic and Social Investigation in Manchester, 1833–1933* (1934), Michael J. Cullen, *The Statistical Movement in Early Victorian Britain. The Foundations of Empirical Social Research* (1975), David Elesh, 'The Manchester Statistical Society: A Case Study of Discontinuity in the History of Empirical Social Research', in A. Oberschall, *The Establishment of Empirical Sociology: Studies in Continuity, Discontinuity and Institutionalization* (1972). Within the history of science considerable historiographical significance has been accorded similarly to the Manchester Literary and Philosophical Society, see A. Thackray, 'Natural Knowledge in Cultural Context: The Manchester Model', *American Historical Review* 79.3 (1974), 672–709, R.H. Kargon, *Science in Victorian Manchester* (1977).

6 Mary Poovey, *Making a Social Body. British Cultural Formation, 1830–1864* (1995), Patrick Joyce, *The Rule of Freedom. Liberalism and the Modern City* (2003), Chris Otter, *The Victorian Eye. A Political History of Light in Britain, 1800–1910* (2008). This Foucauldian interpretation has also been given powerful expression in the context of London by the work of Lyn Nead and Pamela Gilbert, including Nead, *Victorian Babylon. People, Streets and Images in Nineteenth Century London* (2000), Gilbert, *Mapping the Victorian Social Body* (2004), *Cholera and Nation: Doctoring the Social Body in Victorian England* (2008) and her edited collection *Imagined Londons* (2002).

7 Pamela K. Gilbert, 'The Victorian Social Body and Urban Cartography', in Gilbert, ed., *Imagined Londons*, 14.

8 Poovey, *Making*, 31, 15–16, 36; compare L. Nead, 'From Alleys to Courts: Obscenity and the Mapping of mid-Victorian London', *New Formations* 37 (Spring 1999), 33–46, 43, with Poovey's sense of complication of this process in the admission that 'Local circumstances' remain important, 'not merely because specific circumstances posed special problems, but also because in some circumstances, rationalities that pertained to earlier social forms tended to persist and in some cases actually impeded the implementation of abstraction', *Making*, 26. See also the significant influence of James C. Scott's *Seeing Like a State. How Certain Schemes to Improve the Human Condition have Failed* (1998).

9 See as well as the works cited below, Simon Gunn, 'From Hegemony to Governmentality: Changing Perceptions of Power in Social History', *Journal of Social History* 31.2 (2006), 705–20; Matthew Gandy, 'The Bacteriological City and its Discontents', *Historical Geography* 34 (2006), 14–25.

10 Mary Poovey, *A History of the Modern Fact. Problems of Knowledge in the Sciences of Wealth and Society* (1998).

11 Tom Crook, 'Secrecy and Liberal Modernity in Victorian and Edwardian England', in Simon Gunn and James Vernon, eds, *The Peculiarities of Liberal Modernity in Imperial Britain* (2011), 72–90, idem, *Governing Systems. Modernity and the Making of Public Health in England, 1830–1910* (2016). See also Graham

Mooney, *Intrusive Interventions: Public Health, Domestic Space, and Infectious Disease Surveillance in England, 1840–1914* (2015), Matthew L. Newsom Kerr, *Contagion, Isolation, and Biopolitics in Victorian London* (2018).

12 Oz Frankel, *States of Inquiry: Social Investigations and Print Culture in Nineteenth-Century Britain and the United States* (2006), Kathrin Levitan, *A Cultural History of the British Census: Envisioning the Multitude in the Nineteenth Century* (2011).

13 Lauren Goodlad, *Victorian Literature and the Victorian State. Character and Governance in a Liberal Society* (2003); see also Gage McWeeny, *The Comfort of Strangers: Social Life and Literary Form* (2016), Tina Young Choi, *Anonymous Connections: The Body and Narratives of the Social in Victorian Britain* (2016), Emily Steinlight, *Populating the Novel. Literary Form and the Politics of Surplus Life* (2018). See also Michael Klotz, 'Manufacturing Fictional Individuals: Victorian Social Statistics, the Novel, and Great Expectations', *Novel* 46.2 (2013), 214–33.

14 Otter, *Victorian Eye* and also Crook and O'Hara, *Statistics and the Public Sphere*. It is impossible to see this as the 'post-Foucauldian dispensation' which Amanda Anderson and Joseph Valente thought they detected in 2002, *Disciplinarity at the Fin de Siècle* (2002), 8.

15 As in Audrey Jaffe, *The Affective Life of the Average Man. The Victorian Novel and the Stock Market Graph* (2010), and most recently David A.P. Womble, 'Phineas Finn, the Statistics of Character, and the Sensorium of Liberal Personhood', *Novel* 51.1 (2018), 17–35.

16 Kerr, *Biopolitics in Victorian London*, 233.

17 His comment that 'social historians and theorists all too rarely … put the simultaneous conquest of time and space at the center of their concerns', David Harvey, 'Money, Time, Space and the City' in his *The Urban Experience* (1989), 175. Space has remained fashionable, and it is still true to say, as Richard Phillips observed in *Mapping Men and Empire: A Geography of Adventure* (1997), that the current markets 'sell time, buy space', 127. Edward Said, *Culture and Imperialism* (1993), Simon Gikandi's *Maps of Englishness* (1996), Matthew H. Edney, *Mapping an Empire: The Geographical Construction of British India, 1765–1843* (1997).

18 W. Cooke Taylor, 'Objects and Advantages of Statistical Science', *Foreign Quarterly Review* 16 (October 1835), 103–16, quoted by Poovey, *History of the Modern Fact*, 313.

19 Faucher, *Manchester in 1844*, 16; although Faucher does provide a number of geographical references, designed to provide exemplifications of his descriptions ('If you traverse the poor quarters of the town – Angel Meadow, Garden-street, Newtown, St George's Road, Oldham Road, Ancoats, Little Ireland', 27), his emphasis remains on the social cleavage, the gaps between working class and middle class, and hence on the homogeneity of the working-class districts.

20 Andrew Ure, *The Philosophy of Manufactures: or, an Exposition of the Scientific, Moral and Commercial Economy of the Factory System of Great Britain* (1835); ditto for C. Turner Thackrah, *The Effects of the Principal Arts, Trades and Professions , and of Civic States and Habits of Living, on Health...* (2nd edn, 1832). Plus Holland Hoole, *Letter to Lord Althorp in Defence of the Cotton Factories of Lancashire* (1832); John Kennedy, 'Observations on the Influence of Machinery upon the Working Classes of the Community', *Memoirs of the Literary and Philosophical Society of Manchester* 2nd series, V, 25–35.

21 Visible in the work of leading Manchester Statistical Society figures such as John Roberton, as in his 'Report on the Amount and Causes of Death in Manchester', *Royal Commission on State of Large Towns, Second Report*, Appendix II, *PP* (1845), V, 106–16; and D. Noble, *The Influence of Manufacturers on Health* (1843).

22 This provides an even more exaggerated local instance of the Liberal identity that Lawrence Goldman has identified in the National Association for the Promotion of Social Science, *Science, Reform and Politics in Victorian Britain* (2002).

23 There was an important group of 'Liberal Anglicans', including T.C. Horsfall and Herbert Philips active in social reform circles in later Victorian Manchester. But in the earlier period, the sectarian character of the Statistical Society was reflected, for example, in the lack of coverage in the (Conservative) *Manchester Courier* in comparison to for example the activities of the Manchester and Salford Sanitary Association.

24 See references in Note 10. The argument of Elesh, 'Manchester Statistical Society', that statistical movement 'fails' when its energies are diverted into politically divided campaigns such as for education misses the fundamental point that the MSS and its agenda was inherently sectarian from the outset.

25 Editorial, *Manchester City News* (hereafter *MCN*), 23 October 1886.

26 Nor was it the case, as suggested in some quarters, that the cost of paid investigators led to the abandonment of surveys, Schweber, *Disciplining Statistics*, 121.

27 Yeo, *Contest for Social Science*, 75–6, and chapter 3 *passim*.

28 See Richson, 'On the Importance of Statistical and Economical Inquiries', *Transactions of the Manchester Statistical Society* (hereafter *TMSS*), 5 (1857–8), 4.

29 See T. Porter, 'Statistics and the Career of Public Reason: Engagement and Detachment in a Quantified World', in Crook and O'Hara, *Statistics and the Public Sphere*, 32–50.

30 Richard Baron Howard's report 'On the Prevalence of Diseases Arising from Contagion, Malaria and Certain Other Physical Causes amongst the Labouring Classes of Manchester', in *Local Reports on the Sanitary Condition of the Labouring Population of England*, *PP* (1842), XXVII, 294–336; Noble, *Influence of Manufactures on Health*; also John Leigh's paper on the sanitary conditions of Manchester, see *Manchester Guardian* (hereafter *MG*), 9, 16 October 1844.

31 Including J.B. Kirkman's report on the sanitary conditions of Chorlton Union, Ardwick, see *MG*, 15 December 1849; the sanitary conditions of Pendleton, see *MG*, 23 August 1851; T.G. Richmond on the sanitary conditions of Hulme, see *Manchester Examiner and Times* (hereafter *MX*), 11 February 1854. Plus ancillary local surveys, such as William Royston, 'Sanitary State of Ancoats' for the M&SSA, *MX*, 15 March 1854.

32 Royston on the sanitary condition of Ancoats (1854), *MX*, 15 March 1854. In 1860, the rules were altered to give more focus to the role of the association in investigating and publishing information on sanitary questions (see *MX*, 14 February 1860). Thereafter see, for example, A. Ransome and W. Royston, *Report Upon the Health of Manchester and Salford* (1867), J. Leigh, *Report on Infectious Diseases in Manchester* (1871), the M&SSA enquiry into the district bounded by Oldham Road, Addington Street, Angel Street, St Michael's Church Yard, Gas works and Oldham Road Goods station (in St George's District), made by Fred Scott and J. Corbett in February 1877,

which included around 700 back-to-back or single-fronted cottages, as well as others, Manchester City Council, *Proceedings* (hereafter *MCCP*) (1877–8), 262; John Thresh's *An Enquiry into the Causes of the Excessive Mortality in No. 1 District, Ancoats* (1889).

33 For the M&SSA, this included John Leigh, P.H. Holland, Richard Baron Howard and William Gaskell; see the account of Holland in *MG*, 28 May 1845. For Gaskell's role see *Commemoration of the fifty years' ministry of the rev. William Gaskell, M.A.* [1878], 51.

34 See Desrosieres, *Politics of Large Numbers*; Crook, *Governing Systems*.

35 Cited in *Poor Law Commissioners Inquiry into the Sanitary State of the Labouring Population of Great Britain* (1842), XXVII, 155–6. This point is made by Elesh, 'Manchester Statistical Society', 53.

36 A good example is Howard's report 'On the prevalence of diseases ... amongst the labouring classes of Manchester', in which he notes that the records of Manchester's medical institutions were not sufficient to the investigation he had purposed, and he falls back on the authority of his 'above 10 years' constant medical attendance on the poor in Manchester'.

37 James P. Kay-Shuttleworth, *The Moral and Physical Condition of the Working Classes Employed in the Cotton Manufacture in Manchester* (1832), 72, 32.

38 A. Ransome and W. Royston, *Remarks on Some of the Numerical Tests of the Health of Towns* (1863), 6.

39 Levitan, *British Census*, 190–4.

40 Henry Gaulter, *The Origin and Progress of the Malignant Cholera in Manchester* (1833), e.g. 86–7; statement of [Thomas] Dorrington, in the evidence of Rumsey, Q9104, *Select Committee on Medical Poor Relief, Third Report, PP* (1844), IX, 542, compare to Rumsey's endorsement of the comments of Baron Howard on the medical statistics, 560.

41 MSS, *Report on the State of Education in Manchester in 1834* (1835).

42 A. Samelson, *Dwellings and the Death Rate in Manchester* (1883), 34.

43 Adshead, *Distress in Manchester. Evidence (Tabular and Otherwise) of the State of the Labouring Classes in 1840–42* (1842), v, viii.

44 Adshead, *Distress in Manchester*, 25, 20. The 'valuable and unquestioned records' of the town missionaries were used not just for general social conditions, but also for statistics of income, see *ibid*, 19. In his evidence to the 1852–3 Select Committee on Education in Manchester and Salford, Adshead was even more explicit, justifying his use of the MCM missionaries by arguing that their 'peculiar position' and 'constant employment' among the working classes meant that 'they are much better qualified to obtain ... accurate information than indiscriminate stipendiary agency', Q2027 (7 June 1852).

45 'Introduction', David Englander and Rosemary O'Day, *Retrieved Riches. Social Investigation in Britain, 1840–1914* (1995), 7–18.

46 See MH12/6044 1850/106-110, National Archives (hereafter NA). Noble's *Influence of Manufactures upon Health* (1843) was one of the marker texts of the shift from the factory system analyses of the 1830s to the broader urban analyses of the 1840s, but it was based closely on data drawn from the manuscript 'death books' of Manchester township.

47 As is visible in the citation of Mott in his report on Lancashire to the 1842 Sanitary Enquiry, *PP* (1842), XXVII, 242. Alfred Power, the local commissioner for Lancashire, noted that even his returns on the state of housing based on a questionnaire distributed to relieving officers suffered from significant

variations in competence, and could at best be described as 'tolerably correct' 'on the whole', *ibid*, 244.

48 Tom Crook, 'Suspect Figures. Statistics and Public Trust in Victorian England', in Crook and O'Hara, *Statistics and the Public Sphere*, 172.

49 As quoted in Crook, *Governing Systems*, 138, which also discusses the role of Ladies Sanitary Associations.

50 P. Gaskell, *Artisans and Machinery: The Moral and Physical Condition of the Manufacturing Population...* (1836), x. Indeed, there are numerous references to the *Annual Reports* of the Ministry to the Poor, see, 113, 123, 126, 250, 254; viz Adshead, *Distress in Manchester*, 30.

51 William Langton of the DPS and Rev. Richard Parkinson combined in an investigation of three districts reported by Playfair in *Royal Commission on the State of Large Towns. First Report, PP* (1844), XVII, 370–1; for Langton see *MCN*, 1 October 1881.

52 MSS, *Report of a Committee on the State of Education in the Borough of Manchester in 1834* (1835).

53 *Report of a Committee of the Manchester Statistical Society on the Condition of the Working Classes in an Extensive Manufacturing District in 1834, 1835 and 1836* (1838).

54 'Report of the General Board of Health on the Epidemic Cholera of 1848 and 1849', *PP* (1850), especially 105–6, 122.

55 The description of the relieving officer of the Chorlton Union as quoted by Playfair in *Royal Commission on the State of Large Towns. First Report, PP* (1844), XVII, 22–23.

56 The language of the 'visit' was widespread: for Baron Howard, 'The wretched condition of many of the cellars will scarcely be credited by those who have not visited them', *Local Reports, PP* (1842), XXVII, 306. Of course, those responsible for oversight of Sunday Schools were also commonly called 'visitors'. For Leigh see the detailed summary of his report on the sanitary condition of Manchester, presented as based on his work for the Manchester Royal Infirmary and visiting of the poor, *MG*, 9 October 1844.

2 The visiting mode

Visiting as a knowledge technology

The equation of visiting with learning (and knowing) saturates the social literature of nineteenth-century Manchester, and indeed of the condition of England fiction. Elizabeth Gaskell's famous rejection of political economy in her preface to *Mary Barton*, represented not just a gambit of gendered positioning, but a repudiation of the whole epistemological regime of the statistical movement and its anti-clerical overtones.[1] The attention of the Victorian novel shifted from the 1850s, but the symbolic significance of the visit persisted. When the local weekly *The Shadow* attempted an exposé of social conditions in 1870, it was on the 'unvisited slum' that its article focused; unvisited signified not just neglected but also unknown.[2]

Such instances are indicative of the centrality of what we might think of as a 'visiting mode' in the construction of social knowledge in Victorian Manchester, in contradistinction to what might for convenience sake be termed the 'statistical' mode emphasised by others, or indeed a 'royal commission' model of the sort proposed by Oz Frankel.[3] By the 'visiting mode', I intend to mean more than just the traditional form of district visiting, and indeed more than just those individuals or institutions engaged in the broader range of activities which established 'visiterly relations', but those figures who commonly featured in Victorian social description who could be expected to 'penetrate into the working class districts', and who engaged primarily on a house-by-house basis: 'the school board man, the doctor or the city missionary';[4] the tract distributors and scripture readers, visiting ministers of religion, the relieving officers of the Boards of Guardians and sanitary inspectors, and with them the characteristic modes of thinking and argument that these individuals and their activities produced.

Following on from the pioneering work of John Seed, there has been some scholarly recognition of the breadth and significance of visiting.[5] But discussion is still skewed towards female visiting, and while quite rightly stressing the importance of visiting for our understanding of the roles that Victorian women undertook, there is a danger that this focus obscures the wider visiting mode in which women participated. Although visiting was often presented as particularly women's work, it was a responsibility widely undertaken by both men and women. In contrast to the sectionalism of the statistical movement, visiting was marked by its centrality: as much a part of Anglican culture as of Nonconformist; employed widely both by voluntary associations and by the emerging apparatus of the central and local state; philanthropic workers, charitable volunteers, Sunday school teachers, temperance advocates and parochial visitors, supplemented by a corps of predominantly male, paid agents, including town missionaries, scripture readers, ragged school workers, temperance agents and school board visitors.[6] There was a largely hidden economy of paid visitors; William Logan later prominent for his studies of prostitution, was employed for two years in 1840–1841 as a home missionary by Messrs John Bright and Brothers in Rochdale, from where he also visited Manchester.[7] Much of this activity has passed beyond the reach of the historical record, but the numbers involved were substantial. Even allowing for the inevitable fluctuations and failures, the pervasiveness of domestic visiting cannot be doubted.[8] Adshead estimated that 35,000 were being visited in Manchester in 1842.[9] The Manchester City Mission sustained generally 70–80 missionaries through to the end of the century (in contrast to the 15–20 nuisance inspectors employed by the city council, or the handful of medical officers employed by the Board of Guardians, cut from 6 to 3 in the later 1870s).[10] During the 1860s, the Manchester Nurse Training Institute nurses worked closely with the Poor Law relieving officers; in the 1880s, the institute employed around 15 nurses, and by 1900 the number had increased to over 50.[11] In the 1870s, serious consideration was given in some quarters to the introduction into Manchester of the Elberfeld system of visitation and relief, an echo of Thomas Chalmers' Edinburgh schemes of the 1820s.[12] Indeed, in March 1879, the District Provident Society agreed to reconstruct itself to allow focus on systematic district visiting on the Elberfeld model, although ultimately this was only implemented in a small district of Ancoats, and fairly rapidly abandoned.[13] Into the 1880s and 1890s, the visitors of the Ladies Sanitary Association worked as close ancillaries of the city's Medical Officer of Health, but also closely with the clergy, occupying districts coterminous with Anglican parishes, serving under the superintendence of the clergy or their wives, in some cases partly with parochial funding. Although maintaining the machinery of visiting was not easy, in a society wracked with anxieties about social dislocation and experiencing rapid urban growth, the visiting ideal retained enormous purchase.

Visiting did much more than provide 'a feminized epistemology of sympathy', in which the tradition of the mid-century Bible Women is transmitted into the Charity Organisation Society and the Salvation Army.[14] Work in visiting organisations provided the authority to speak on social matters, as was the case for the housing reformer Octavia Hill, or the Manchester cotton merchant William O'Hanlon, leading promoter of provident dispensaries in the 1870s and 1880s, and a ragged school worker in Ancoats from 1861,[15] or Charles E.B. Russell, one of the late Victorian pioneers of youth work, and volunteer at the Heyrod-Street Mission Hall in Manchester.[16] Russell's major works were published later, but he was an active presence in public debate on social matters in Manchester throughout the 1890s. Even unaffiliated missionaries like the Unitarian Travers Madge were seen as natural interlocutors of the social condition of the poor.[17]

Despite the stereotyped and conventionally religious nature of much of its literature,[18] visiting established itself as by far the most important Victorian technology of social knowledge. The difficulty of casual admission to the working-class home was recognised even as the inspecting functions of central and local state were extended, and visiting associations were prized precisely for their ability to break down obstacles both of access and of interpretation.[19] The experience of visiting could have a lasting impact on the visitor; Charles Rowley, whose later organisation of the Ancoats Brotherhood brought him to national prominence, was powerfully affected, even as someone born and brought up in Ancoats, by his visiting experiences during the cotton famine of the 1860s.[20] And although generally subordinate to some primary task of education, reformation or relief, the collection of information in some sort of systematic way was almost universally part of the visitors' role.[21] The possibility of taking advantage of their normal routines to collect information in at least a semi-regular form was a natural progression for conscientious visitors.[22] It was normal for paid agents to maintain a diary, even if this is not always readily apparent from published accounts. Visitors often maintained extremely comprehensive and systematic records of information elicited in the course of their visits.[23] This was true of home missionaries like James Bembridge, an unaffiliated district visitor employed by a local manufacturer, Thomas Crewdson, to serve a portion of the factory district of Ancoats, as well as of the visitors of the Ladies Sanitary Association.[24] Advice manuals for volunteer visitors routinely recommended the keeping of some sort of journal, and often offered complicated suites of report and recommendation forms for visiting societies to use in the recording of information covering at least religious affiliations, schooling, employment, wages and rent.[25] At times, even contemporaries worried that the manuals suggested an overly investigative stance; it was noted that Hill had to work to prevent the Charity Organisation Society from becoming 'a dry, ineffectual machinery for enquiring about people'.[26]

Such concerns notwithstanding, visiting societies functioned as an apparatus to be exploited, furnishing the machinery for local surveys and supplying 'informants' for externally sponsored social investigations, a considerable number of which were published during the Victorian period.[27] Even during the height of the statistical moment in the 1830s onwards, contemporary debate relied extensively on the evidence of visitors.[28] Visiting societies continued to support the intermittent investigative work of the MSS. Fred Scott's enquiry into 'The Condition and Occupations of the People of Manchester and Salford' presented to the Statistical Society in 1889 drew heavily on information provided by the 'mission women' of the Ladies Sanitary Association, and the Ministry to the Poor, and he was a strong advocate of the collaboration of visiting societies in the collection of information and the organisation of social investigations.[29] Visitors acted as guides to interested outsiders, as John Layhe, of the Unitarian Ministry to the Poor, did for the Swedish writer Frederica Bremer during her visit to Manchester in 1851.[30] Into the 1890s, professional investigators despatched to Manchester by central government were seeking and receiving the guidance of local visitors.[31]

Throughout the period, parochial visiting societies and the like provided the mechanism for local surveys, as well as seeking to provide descriptions of working-class culture inflected with respectable moral outrage. Examples include St Andrew's Society for the Promotion of Christian Knowledge collecting and publishing statistics on education in Ancoats in 1839.[32] Manchester City Mission missionaries surveyed their districts not just for religious belief and attendance, but also for school attendance,[33] for visits to public houses, for the extent of Sunday trading.[34] The Redbank Christian Total Abstinence Bible Class, which maintained regular visiting and tract distribution, surveyed the 24 streets at the heart of the Red Bank district in 1861, reporting on the balance of cellars and houses, the range of rents and the number of public houses and beerhouses.[35] There were still examples of parochial visiting–based survey work at the very end of the period, such as the census on religion covering 15,000 homes conducted by Nonconformist groups in South Manchester in 1899.[36] Even where existing visitors were not used and visiting was not itself a pivotal activity, surveys employed their own special 'visitors', and voluntary associations offered a reservoir of willing labour. In 1850, the Cobdenite social reformer John Watts urged that the Manchester and Salford Temperance Society divide the town into districts, to which visitors would be appointed to collect statistics of the circumstances, habits and character of the population.[37]

The Manchester and Salford Sanitary Association epitomises this configuration. It sought at its outset to operate by means of a series of local 'visiting committees', designed to have an educative purpose, but primarily to facilitate the collection of information about social and sanitary conditions, producing a comprehensive series of reports on Manchester, district by district.[38] Tellingly, the list of 'persons … whom it is desirable' to have on these committees was headed by clergymen and ministers of religion, and included, after members of the medical profession, architects, surveyors and registrars of births and deaths, 'the town missionaries, scripture readers and district visitors' and 'teachers of day and Sunday schools'.[39] The Sanitary Association collaborated with John Layhe, and later sought to co-operate with the Manchester City Mission by giving special lectures on sanitary matters to Bible Women associated with the mission.[40] And although the district committees had largely fallen into disuse by the late 1850s, ties to the culture of visiting were restored in the 1860s through the formation of the Ladies Sanitary Association, itself committed to the appointment of 'sanitary women' who, under the supervision of middle-class 'ladies', and frequently supervised and funded by Anglican parishes, visited the homes of the poor, offering advice and cleaning materials, while also collecting information.

Visiting epistemologies

Of course, visiting was more than just a technology for the accumulation of information. It also encouraged a number of particular epistemological assumptions about the constitution of social knowledge, a specific set of investigative methodologies and a repertoire of rhetorical strategies.

The literature of the visiting associations produced powerfully stylised texts which employed a range of conventional tropes and stock characters (the wilful atheist, the careless drunkard, the struggling widow), but often offered little in the way of direct social description. Indeed, there was some tension between its purported realism and the extent to which its substance was often borrowed, reworked or perhaps even entirely imaginary.[41] Frequently, however, even the most stylised conversion literature adopted a realist address (the mechanics of the visiting mode, the dated journal entry), and deployed claims to local knowledge to affirm its authority. At the heart of these generic imperatives was an 'ethnographic' mode which privileged observation and 'impression' and those social facts which could be seen, and marginalised elements of social circumstance that could not be observed (often, as in the case of wage levels and occupational circumstances, despite their central importance).[42] C.S. Loch of the Charity Organisation Society told his diary that 'To be a naturalist in social matters is right',[43] and Layhe repeatedly bolstered his claims to authoritative status by affirming, for example, that he 'write[s] from facts which I have repeatedly witnessed'.[44] This 'visiting epistemology' in turn encouraged particular 'forms' of knowledge, a specific set of generic imperatives which we might render as exploration, the encounter, the tableau and the specimen or the case. These forms were not exclusive: to a greater or lesser extent, they shade into those found in other forms of nineteenth-century social description.[45] But their operation as crucial framing devices helped both characterise a particular mode of engagement and shape the nature of the knowledge it produced.

The spatial overtones of these treatments should not be underestimated. Social realities were occluded: commenting on the problem of 'unrecognised tenement dwellings', the Manchester Diocesan Conference *Report on Housing* of 1902 noted that 'They do not show to the eye. They are only known to us by conscientious house-to-house visitation'.[46] As a result, as Alan Mayne and others have noted, visiting accounts often commenced with an act of 'penetration'. The motif of movement from familiar thoroughfare to mysterious and threatening inner district was widely used. Slum workers 'plunge into the lowest depths of the city',[47] accessing locales possible only with the help of a guide, and probably protector.[48] Movement from street to residence was tracked by itineraries down narrow passages, blind alleys, courts within courts. And although the doorways of working-class residences were routinely populated with the idle and dissolute, sitting on steps or lounging in doorways in a transgressive blurring of the public and the private, it is noticeable that many of the actual encounters of this literature required further incursion through to back rooms or up flights of rickety stairs to cramped garrets. After exploration came encounter. As well as serving the overarching visiting narrative of 'resistance overcome', the encounter rooted description and identified its subjects with their particular setting, as cellar-, court- or attic-dwellers. As the century progressed, the locations of these encounters tended to proliferate: not just home, but street, public house, mission hall and even chapel. But even here the structure of the meeting was almost invariably directed towards the domestic, both as a source of identity and a site of contact. The primary effects sought here were admittedly merely obscurity and distance; but this of itself helped to reinforce, albeit without specificity, spatialised understandings of social conditions, and as these accounts were generally placed, even if only in the vaguest terms ('off Deansgate'), they contributed in turn to broader cartographic conceptions of the city.

While on the surface such conceptions sit easily with formulations of surveillance/knowledge/power, in practice, they inscribed less a claim to authority than a recognition of the limits of documentary and especially quantitative information, derived from a sense that words themselves were inadequate (to, for example, 'wretchedness that cannot possibly be described' as Samuel Robinson, another Unitarian Minister to the Poor, put it),[49] from an unwillingness to accept the reductionism associated with classification schemas, and from a persistent refusal to allow tabular returns to stand as anything more than an affectation of reality.[50] Far from being assured that adequate knowledge could be imparted by expert summary, readers were very often urged to go and see and judge for themselves. As Buckland put it, 'I do wish that, instead of writing reports, what I see and do could be brought before the personal observation of my friends'.[51] These assumptions are apparent even in the more sociological studies appearing at the very end of the century. Hence, T.R. Marr, in his *Housing Conditions in Manchester and Salford* (1904), in introducing one tabulation of water supplies conceded that 'The figures given in this table give some idea of the state of affairs, though only a personal inspection of the streets and of the taps can give a true picture'.[52]

Reports of visitors and missionaries constantly resorted to the presentation of tableaux, or as the author of *Manchester at Night: Its Sins and Suffering* (1885) put it, 'glimpses' of city life, 'by which the readers saw what our Missionaries were constantly seeing'.[53] In the same way, the journalism of social conditions, even when the authors themselves were clearly outsiders and not visitors, recurred repeatedly to the visiting devices of tour, visit, sketch and conversation. The author of the series 'On the Social Condition of the Working Classes of Manchester', published in the *Manchester Examiner and Times* in 1852 began having selected a street, 'being accompanied by a friend who frequently calls to see them [later fairly clearly identified as a MCM missioner], we entered a dark and dirty passage, climbed several old and decaying stairs.... [and] knocked at a door'. While a second article offered a set of 'statistical facts' about the district (apparently furnished by the city missioner), the following article (in consciousness of the 'somewhat general nature' of the previous article) offers a series of 'illustrations ... furnished by cases'. Expressly not 'tales of romance and excitement' but 'simple sketches of the life which we find in the cellars, garrets and rooms into which we make our way'.[54] Late Victorian newspaper coverage is saturated with this sort of approach, both in its features and in its letter columns.[55]

This semiotic sociology did not preclude eliciting testimony from inhabitants; not only did it offer a framework for the administration of surveys or questionnaires, but it was also valued as providing a built-in check on the accuracy and reliability of any information proffered. Visitors were used to a greater or lesser extent throughout the period to ask questions about denominational identity and attendance at worship. There was understandable interest in attempting to elicit information about household incomes and expenditures (especially on rent, and on the balance between essential and 'luxury' purchases). At times, more sophisticated catalogues of questions were attempted. One micro-enquiry of 1889 sought to obtain information about occupations, weekly rents, number and size of rooms in each house, the general condition of the home, the number in the family, including the number of children under 13, of lodgers, the character of any work or trade carried on in the house and any illness and causes thereof.[56] But, in general, there was a lack of confidence in the testimony of the observed, and limited opportunity for the objects of enquiry to speak for themselves except in closely controlled and editorialised environments.[57] Peter Gaskell insisted in his *Artisans and Machinery: The Moral and Physical Condition of the Manufacturing Population* (1836), 'the operatives cannot be supposed to judge fairly of their condition'.[58] The Manchester Statistical Society reports of the 1860s are, ironically, perhaps the most obvious example of the willingness of investigators to accumulate and represent quantifications based on information provided by householders and occupants.[59]

Tabulated arithmetic data was not entirely precluded. But where statistics were used, they tended to be subsequent to impressionistic accounts. Indeed, the sort of categorisation and quantification of impression which was a feature of early Victorian statistical texts, was entirely consonant with elements of the visiting mode, although almost always of the visitor rather than the visited.[60] When by the mid-1890s the increasingly bureaucratised visitors of the Ladies Sanitary Association were providing the raw data for a series of statistical tables that James Niven, Manchester's Medical Officer of Health, was publishing in his quarterly returns, these were predominantly aggregations of impressions as to whether the house was 'dilapidated', 'dirty', 'improved' or 'overcrowded', as much judgements about respectability as about material circumstances.[61] But, in general, doubts about the reduction of a range of specific circumstances to a numerical series predominated. John Layhe spoke for many in commenting that mere quantification of the number of visits was meaningless, given the variability and importance of the quality of each visit: 'So much depends on the spirit in which an act is done and received, that no verbal statement of its having been performed any number of times can express its moral value'.[62] Even Kay-Shuttleworth spoke of municipal reports of the 1850s and early 1860s as being 'deformed with an accumulation of statistics'.[63] Instead, visiting was marked by a particularising instinct which affirmed the belief that knowledge came from comprehending individual circumstances, not from categorisation.[64] As Gilbert has pointed out, a figure like Octavia Hill eschewed counting for 'numbering' in the biblical sense, for knowing as individuals.[65] Frankel has identified similar assumptions underpinning the activities of parliamentary commissions of inquiry. Visiting played a primary role in embedding this approach.

Where visiting literature proceeded beyond direct description of what could be seen, it did so largely on the basis of the multiplication of individual cases, of the sort already cited from Adshead's *Distress in Manchester* and the staple of the accounts of city missionaries and other visitors.[66] Explicit use of the concept of 'specimen' was widespread.[67] This was more than just a resort to the anecdotal.[68] Nor is it entirely satisfactory to comprehend it, as Maeve Adams does, in terms of 'affective aggregation' in which an exemplary instance, or set of instances, operates metonymically to represent the whole population.[69] Rather, there are parallels here with John Pickstone's analysis of the contemporary medical sociology of knowledge, which he sees as dominated by 'analytical (or museological) science' based on the display, examination and placing of the 'specimen'.[70] In both cases, the assumption was that information was to be obtained and imparted by cumulation rather than calculation, by dissection and differentiation rather than by aggregation.[71]

Significantly, this did not lead to any widespread imitation of Le Play's procedure of in-depth study of a very small number of cases, an approach not common until the twentieth century.[72] The apparent barriers to this approach in Britain are instructive. Yeo's suggestion that 'There was no question of sampling. Completeness was mandatory',[73] is not entirely borne out – the scale of the challenge of Manchester meant that various forms of selectivity were employed by local investigations, albeit more usually those which did not involve door-to-door survey work (and often tellingly using geographical division as the sampling mode).[74] But the aspiration of comprehensive coverage, at least of the working-class component of the population, was established in the initial Statistical Society investigations and never really abandoned. This was encouraged by the underlying assumption that the meaning of individual instances was inflected by their location. The placing of accounts in a recognisable geography sharpened their sense of realism and offered a resonance of authenticity.[75] But it did more: unlike the homogenisation encouraged by the 'explorer' mode, rather than efface local and district particularity, the visiting mode encouraged precise geographical delineation and differentiation, considered and – if necessary – classified in situ.[76] For data developed in this context, the concept of distribution was over-determinedly spatial and not statistical.

The territorialisation of Victorian social knowledge

We should not overlook the significance of the explicitly territorial nature of all visiting institutions; visitors generally had a 'district' and mode of reporting which encouraged them to identify its particularities, in which the gaze, far from being abstracted, as Joyce has argued, remained intensely personalised and situated. Visiting information was almost invariably placed even when not plotted, and rather than serving to efface geographic distinction and render space isotropic, involved a process of location. Even the statistical accounts of the 1830s and 1840s weren't able to escape this entirely. Kay-Shuttleworth's own experience as medical officer for the Ancoats and Ardwick Dispensary made him acutely sensitive – despite a surface rhetoric of 'dense masses of habitations of the poor' – to the varied character of the districts of the city, and the particular problems presented by areas such as the Irish 'ghetto' known as 'Little Ireland', or the notorious riverside slum of 'Gibralter'.[77] Admittedly, the development of state information gathering based on registration or census districts meant that where in the statistical literature of the 1830s data was broken down geographically, it was almost always into these largely artificial divisions, rather than as an attempt to delineate the precise boundaries of social conditions. Nevertheless, even in these texts, social description often involved the development of moral topographies which 'constituted the town as a field of distribution' of social phenomena by mapping them onto actual rather than Euclidian space.[78]

It does seem entirely counter-intuitive to argue that the early Victorian period saw the flattening out of social space. After all, it was not visiting alone that was encouraging the territorialisation of social understandings. Civil registration data broken down into registration districts, census material in enumeration districts and the starkly uneven spatial distribution of cholera deaths all helped create new spatialised forms of social knowledge.[79] The dominance of the sanitary over the medical, the miasmatic over the epidemiological, further encouraged attention to overcrowded locations rather than social vectors of transmission.[80] Similarly, although historical geographers have long debated the precise extent of social segregation, there is no doubt that the second quarter of the century witnessed a middle-class flight to the suburbs, and intensified anxieties about the isolation of working-class districts.[81] The reliance of the working classes on foot transport tied them to housing close to their places of work, helping to give character to particular districts and placed visible strains on an institutional fabric which had very often to be organised locally, in municipal wards and townships, police beats or Anglican parishes. Hence the comment of one resident of Ancoats in 1857: 'I live in the middle of an immense population in Mill-street. The library in Campfield is two miles from my house, and having long hours to work its abounding shelves and beautiful rooms might as well be twenty miles away for any use they are to me'.[82] Social provision such as wash houses, it was observed, needed to be 'sprinkled generously throughout these congested districts'.[83] The expansion of the population, especially in the first two thirds of the century, created a never-ending cycle of new districts with fast-growing populations in need of civic amenities and institutions.

In fact, most Victorian social and philanthropic activity was territorial, its operations were focused on particular districts, or its city-wide presence was sought through district organisation. Territorial possessiveness was often just below the surface, especially among the Anglican clergy. Edward Brotherton observed even in the 1860s that it had been intimated to him that 'it was considered presumptuous' for him to have gone visiting the poor in certain districts 'without asking for permission in certain quarters'.[84] Municipal sanitary inspection was organised on a district basis through to the end of the century.[85] Even state institutions like the Poor Law operated at times in quite rigidly territorial ways: unions were divided into districts, in which the relevant local officers were required to reside without exception, even when circumstances made this problematic.[86] Reliance on visiting encouraged such conceptions. Because visiting organisations were not comprehensive and tended to focus on the areas of greatest need, such solidarities encouraged the tendency of social description to concentrate on a few particularly notorious areas, at times relatively detached from their situation in the overall urban system.[87] In this sense, visiting created a knowledge less invested in the interrelations of different locations and their inhabitants, in, for example, modes and practices of movement across the city, than in the internal characteristics and dynamics of locality. The Manchester and Salford City Mission (MCM) provides a powerful illustration. From the outset, the published accounts of its home missionary activity adopted an insistent topographic rhetoric, the 'worst districts', the neglected portions of the town, in which local context loomed large: the impact of neighbours, the configurations of local recreations, the particular pattern of religious provision.[88] There was a hesitancy about transparent identification of specific districts, but this was largely stylistic: accounts frequently contained more than enough detail to fix exact locations.[89]

Notes

1 Robert Gray, *The Factory Question and Industrial England* (1996), 154–5.
2 'An Unvisited Slum', *The Shadow* (1869–70), 323–4; compare the similar usage in the quotation in A. Mayne, *The Imagined Slum: Newspaper Representation in Three Cities, 1870–1914* (1983), 136–7.
3 Frankel, *States of Inquiry.*
4 Walter Tomlinson, *Bye-Ways of Manchester Life* (1887), 64. Compare with the *Birmingham Daily Gazette*'s 1883 reference to 'earnest philanthropists, parish doctors, clergymen and district visitors', see Mayne, *Imagined Slum*, 136.
5 John Seed, 'Unitarianism, Political Economy and the Antinomies of Liberal Culture in Manchester, 1830–50', *Social History* 7 (1982), 1–25, also F.K. Prochaska, *Women and Philanthropy in Nineteenth Century England* (1980); Monica Correa Fryckstedt, '*Mary Barton* and the *Reports of the Ministry to the Poor*: A New Source', *Studia Neophilologica* 50 (1980), 333–6; Deborah Carlin, '"What Methods Have Brought Blessing": Discourses of Reform

in Philanthropic Literature', in Joyce Warner, ed., *The (Other) American Traditions* (1993), 203–25; Celia Davies, 'The Health Visitor as Mother's Friend: A Woman's Place in Public Health, 1900–14', *Social History of Medicine* 1.1 (1988), 39–59. See also, J.R. Walkowitz, *City of Dreadful Delight.*
Narratives of Sexual Danger in Late Victorian London (1992), Vanessa Heggie, 'Health Visiting and District Nursing in Victorian Manchester; Divergent and Convergent Vocations', *Women's History Review* 20.3 (2011), 403–22; Seth Koven, *Slumming. Sexual and Social Politics in Victorian London* (2004), 57ff, and most recently Thomas R.C. Gibson-Bryden, 'Women and Charity: Love, Feminism and "Men's Worlds"', in his *Moral Mapping of Edwardian London. Charles Booth, Christian Charity and the Poor-but-Respectable* (2018).

6 For the intermittent activity of the temperance movement see Martin Hewitt, 'The Travails of District Visiting: Manchester 1830–1870', *Historical Research* 71 (1998), 208. For ragged school works, see the account of John Armstrong, Jnr, visiting 70 families weekly in Angel Meadow, in Joseph Johnson, *Heroines of our Times. Sketches* (1860), 211.

7 W. Logan, *The Great Social Evil: Its Causes, Extent, Results and Remedies* (1871), 35–6.

8 Hewitt, 'Travails of District Visiting', 196–227.

9 Adshead, *Distress*, 25, cited Seed, 'Antinomies', 15.

10 See the summary of R.W. Guilmette's second annual report, *MCN*, 3 September 1892.

11 See Manchester Nurse Training Institution, *Annual Report* (1866–7), 13–14, and subsequent reports; Mary Stocks, *A Hundred Years of District Nursing* (1960).

12 See *MCN*, 29 March 1879.

13 *MG*, 4 March 1880. A more sustained effort was made in Liverpool in the 1880s, see A.F. Young and E.T. Ashton, *British Social Work in the Nineteenth Century* (1956), 88–90.

14 For an example of this sort of dismissiveness, see Frankel, *States of Inquiry*, 152. Poovey, *Making*, 43; as quoted by, for example, Ellen Ross, *Slum Travellers: Ladies and London Poverty, 1860–1920* (2007), 14.

15 Letter of O'Hanlon, *MG*, 20 November 1878. O'Hanlon was active in a number of reforming movements in later Victorian Manchester, including the Manchester and Salford Provident Dispensaries Association; see Martin Hewitt, 'Fifty Years Ahead of Its Time? The Provident Dispensaries Movement in Manchester, 1871–1885', in Alan Kidd and Melanie Tebbutt, eds, *Essays in Honour of Mike Rose* (2017), 84–108; *MG*, 24 November 1911, 28 August 1912; *MCN*, 7 September 1912.

16 For Russell, see F.P. Gibbon, 'C.E.B. Russell', in R.S. Forman, ed., *Great Christians* (1933), 483–98. For one example of a social reformer and activist recruited by knowledge acquired as a Sunday School visitor, see Thomas Johnson, long-time worker with the Charter Street ragged school, *MG*, 7 September 1877; cited in 'Alsatia Revisited', *MG*, 1 August 1887.

17 See Elizabeth Gaskell to unknown correspondent, 2 July 1862, in John Chapple and Arthur Pollard, *The Letters of Mrs Gaskell* (1966), 677.

18 Take something like Fred Hirst's *The Slums of Manchester* (1888).

19 For some of the issues involved, and the ways in which visiting literature tended to obscure the partial nature of its access, see Hewitt, 'Travails'.

20 'I can never get out of my inner consciousness the appalling stinks of the cellar dwellings I then visited', C. Rowley, *Fifty Years of Ancoats Loss and*

Gain (1897), 8. Note that even for him, born and brought up in Ancoats, 'it was a revelation'.

21 This had been established at the outset, see A. Twells, *The Civilising Mission and the English Middle Class, 1792–1850: The 'Heathen' at Home and Overseas* (2008), 69–76 (while also noting that it was only with the shift to the domestic mission societies of the 1830s that this statistical interest systematically shifted to material rather than merely moral conditions, *ibid*, 172–3).

22 This determination, after a considerable period of visiting, is visible in Bembridge, 'Journal', 20 January 1850 and the following months. For Bembridge, see the collection of his journals, BR Ms 259.BI, Manchester Archives.

23 For example, the visiting book of Abraham Hume, discussed in Bosworth, 'Hume', 76–7.

24 See 'The Sanitary Mission Woman', *Meliora* XII (1869), 88–9.

25 See, for example, Rev. E.J. Nixon, *A Manual of District Visiting* (1848), 'District Visiting Society', in R. Simpson, *The Clergyman's Manual* (1842), 188–200; printed record books included Rev. R.B. Exton, *Parochial Minister's Assistant* (various editions 1820–39).

26 Quoted Goodlad, *Victorian State*, 115. See the doubts expressed at the recommendations of A.D. Hinton, *Aids to Parochial Visiting*, in respect of enquiries about income, in a review in *The Literary Churchman* V (1859). For a study of a particularly systematic version of this, see Lucy E. Bosworth, 'Home Missionaries to the Poor: Abraham Hume and Spiritual Destitution in Liverpool, 1847–1884', *Transactions of the Lancashire and Cheshire Antiquarian Society* 143 (1993), 57–83, W.S.F. Pickering, 'Abraham Hume (1814–1884): A Forgotten Pioneer of Religious Sociology', *Archives de Sociologie des Religions* 33 (January–June 1972), 33–48.

27 For the important distinction between modes of enquiry, and the argument that the Victorian model was predominantly that of the 'informant', see Catherine Marsh, 'Informants, Respondents and Citizens', in M. Bulmer, ed., *Essays on the History of British Sociological Research* (1985), 206–27.

28 Letter of W.C. Kirkham on the state of Ancoats: from evidence of visitors associated with Every-st Independent Chapel he could 'quite easily prove that contrary to oft repeated assertion, Every-st district is not a "needy and morally destitute district"', *Manchester and Salford Advertiser*, 27 October 1838. See also the statistics on cellars presented at the Manchester City Mission annual general meeting, *Manchester Courier* (hereafter *MC*), 15 June 1839; or the report in *MC*, 24 April 1847, of the City Mission revealing the extent of hidden distress in Manchester.

29 F. Scott, 'The Condition and Occupations of the People of Manchester and Salford', *TMSS* 35 (1888–9), 93–116, and *idem*, 'The Need for Better Organisation of Benevolent Effort in Manchester and Salford', *TMSS* 31 (1884–5), 148–9.

30 *Ministry to the Poor, Annual Report* (hereafter *MTPAR*) (1852), 56.

31 Hence, when Clara Collett visited Manchester (as one of the inspectors of the Labour Department) in 1893 to get information on conditions in Jewish workshops, she appeared, according to the *Lancet* 'to have received valuable assistance from the district visitors [from the Ladies Society for Visiting the Jewish Poor] in her inquiries…', *Lancet* (January–June 1893), 1288.

32 *MC*, 23 November 1839. And if not lay visitors, then the clergy themselves, as in the survey of three Manchester parishes by clergymen noted by John Watts, 'Fifteen Years of School Board Work in Manchester', *TMSS* 32 (1885–6), 114.

33 For example, Manchester City Mission, *Annual Report* (hereafter *MCMAR*) (1844), 6; *Manchester City Mission Magazine* (hereafter *MCMMag*) (February 1853), 1, 5–6, 9; (February 1854), 92.

34 See the detailed report of the canvas carried out in 1860 by the New Cross Lord's Day Observance Society, *MCMMag* (April 1860), 9–10 (including tables). The 1869 Select Committee on the State of Beerhouses includes reports of opinions of MCM missionaries as to the opinions of the Manchester working class, see Q3563.

35 *MG* 2 January 1861; the 1857 Sunday School canvass *MX*, 27 April 1857. Hewitt St Ragged Day School in 1866, *MG*, 21 February 1866. For another parochial survey, see E.B. Chalmers, *The Parson, the Parish and the Working Man* (1859), 6–7.

36 *Manchester Congregational Monthly* (February 1900).

37 John Watts, *MX*, 12 October 1850. See also Select Committee on Public Houses, evidence of William Howarth, Q2007. The Manchester and Salford Temperance Association did undertake some survey work, including its 1854 survey of Sunday drinking, see James Kay-Shuttleworth, *Four Periods of Public Education as Reviewed in 1832–1839–1846–1862* (1862), 133–6.

38 See Manchester and Salford Sanitary Association, *Hints on District Visiting. Tract Series No. 6*, Scrapbook of Printed Items, Manchester and Salford Sanitary Association Papers, M126/5/1/37, Manchester Archives. For its adverts for voluntary visitors, see *MX*, 11 February 1854.

39 M&SSA, 'Instructions for Visiting Committees', Scrapbook of Printed Items, M&SSA Papers, M126/5/1/5, Manchester Archives.

40 *MTPAR* (1854), 16; M&SSA *Annual Report* (1864), 15.

41 There are clear parallels with approaches to photography, as discussed in Koven, *Slumming*, 94–9.

42 Hence, there was virtually no examination after the 1830s of rates of wages (although one of the education inquiries sponsored by the Church party in Manchester in mid-century surveyed 777 families for wage levels among other things; see Richson's evidence to the *Select Committee on Education in Manchester and Salford*, Q492-93). Exceptions are David Chadwick, *On the Rates of Wages in Manchester and Salford [Paper presented to the London Statistical Society, 1859]* (1860); *idem, The Expenditure of Wages, 1839–1887. Read at the British Association, Manchester Meeting, Section F, Monday 5th September 1887* (1887). There was very little attempt to assess the levels of employment or unemployment before the Edwardian period.

43 Quoted Sandra M. Den Otter, *British Idealism and Social Explanation* (1996), 72, in section headed 'Social Explanation by Observation'.

44 *MTPAR* (1851), 20.

45 See Maeve E. Adams, 'Numbers and Narratives: Epistemologies of Aggregation in British Statistics and Social Realism, c.1790–1880', in Crook and O'Hara, *Statistics and the Public Sphere*, 103–20. Of course, this was not exclusively a feature of the visiting mode; it was also a common trope of the 'social topographers' and social explorers of the 1850s and 1860s, like Henry Mayhew and Hector Gavin, see J.A. Yelling, *Slums and Slum Clearance in Victorian London* (1986); and it shares in the dynamics discussed by Daniel Siegel, *Charity and Condescension: Victorian Literature and the Dilemmas of Philanthropy* (2012).

46 *Report ... Housing of the Poor*, 5.

47 *Earnest Work in a Big City* (1886), 28.

48 For example, J.W. MacGill, *Manchester at Night. Its Sins and Sufferings* (1886).
49 *MTPAR* (1866), 21. Patrick Joyce has drawn different but congruent implications from what he describes as the 'paroxysms of moral outrage' that mark public health inspectors reports, 'a revulsion that the inspectors felt was almost impossible within the bounds of decent language to give expression to', Joyce, *Rule of Freedom*, 68.
50 In this sense, one cannot credibly argue as Matthew G. Hannah does in *Governmentality and the Mastery of Territory in Nineteenth-Century America* (2000), 29, that this period saw the stabilisation of the association between precision and accuracy or indeed the forging of a link between numbers and the credibility of their users.
51 *MTPAR* (1841), 9.
52 T.R. Marr, *Housing Conditions in Manchester and Salford* (1904), 61. This echoes the sentiment of the challenge of Bishop Doyle to Nassau Senior cited in Frankel, *States of Inquiry*, 143.
53 J.W. MacGill and Mrs Arthur Weigall, *Seeking and Saving. Being the Rescue Work of the Manchester City Mission* (1889), 15. Compare, *Afternoons in the Manchester Slums. By A Lady* (1887), 'We often hear of these things, but nothing can bring them before us in their realistic aspect but the visiting such places and seeing for ourselves', 13.
54 *MX*, 14, 21, 28 January 1852. For a virtually identical approach see Edwin Waugh's 'Among the Preston Operatives', in his *Home-Life of the Lancashire Factory Folk During the Cotton Famine* (1867), 23–131.
55 To give just one example, the letter of O'Hanlon, *MG*, 20 November 1878, which justifies its position by a description of 'a few visits I made ...one evening this week', with its absolutely characteristic account of rooms bereft of furniture, possessions etc.
56 Thresh, *Report*, 7.
57 A point made by Thresh in 1889 – tenants questioned will in some cases have suspected that evidence was being collected to form the basis for formal proceedings to reduce overcrowding, and so will have underestimated the level of occupancy, Thresh, *Report*.
58 Gaskell, *Artisans and Machinery*, ix.
59 See Henry C. Oats, 'Inquiry into the Educational and Other Conditions of a District in Deansgate', *Transactions of the Manchester Statistical Society* (1864–5), 1–13. This can be contrasted with the approach of Mayhew, see Anne Humpherys, *Travels into the Poor Man's Country. The Work of Henry Mayhew* (1977), 48.
60 T. Wyke and A. Kidd, *The Challenge of Cholera: Proceedings of the Manchester Special Board of Health 1831–1833* (2010).
61 *MCN*, 3 December 1892, 3 March 1894 (citing Tatham's *Quarterly Report*, 2 June 1894); hence, the willingness to mix value judgement and counting noted by Porter, 'Statistics and the Career of Public Reason', as representing the Victorians' 'different sense of the requirements of objectivity', 39.
62 *MTPAR* (1846), 5. Likewise in treating the impact of his Sunday School, he commented that 'mere number is certainly no criterion', *ibid*, 11.
63 Kay-Shuttleworth, *Four Periods*, 94.
64 Hence, Octavia Hill's argument for the part-time visitor, rather than the professional visitor, 'the weary worker, whose life tends to make her deal with people *en masse*', Octavia Hill, *District Visiting. A Few Words to Volunteer Visitors among the Poor* (1876), 5.

65 Pamela K. Gilbert, *The Citizen's Body. Desire, Health and the Social in Victorian England* (2007), 104.
66 See the Manchester City Mission, *Annual Report, Manchester City Mission Magazine, passim.*
67 For example, *MTPAR* (1844), 12; *MCMMag* (May 1853), including the 16th Annual Report, 16.
68 As, for example, in Carolyn Vellenga Berman, '"Awful Unknown Quantities": Addressing the Readers in *Hard Times*', *Victorian Literature and Culture* 37.2 (September 2009), 561–82.
69 Adams, 'Numbers and Narratives', 114–15.
70 For example the shift from Linnaean botany to a stress on plant organisation, functional relations and patterns of organisation, in turn linked to the emergence of statistical analysis in the 1830s, was by the end of the century being replaced in turn by experimental knowledge derived from professionalised scientists based in university laboratories, J.V. Pickstone, 'Ways of Knowing: Toward a Historical Sociology of Science, Technology and Medicine', *British Journal for the History of Science* 26 (December 1993), 433–58. See also the discussion in Gibson-Bryden, *Moral Mapping of Edwardian London*, of what he describes as a dominant Whewellian view: 'to deal "inductively" with moral sciences' by 'build[ing] up hundreds of examples of human conduct .... "observing and classifying phenomena, from which [one] deduces consequences that are ... *in the place of moral laws*"', 28, citing Boyd Hilton quoting Whewell to Richard Jones, 25 February 1831.
71 This was quite different to Le Play's method of in-depth study of a few households, in that their function was primarily communicative rather than constitutive, to embody reality for the reader rather than constructing it for the investigator; hence the delay until Geddes in the championing of Le Play in Britain; see P. Rabinow, *French Modern: Norms and Forms of the Social Environment* (1989).
72 See Rabinow, *French Modern*, 82–3, D. Matless, 'Regional Surveys and Local Knowledges: The Geographical Imagination in Britain, 1918–39', *Transactions of the Institute of British Geographers* ns 17 (1992), 464–80.
73 Eileen Yeo, 'Social Surveys in the 18th and 19th Centuries', in Theodore Porter and Dorothy Ross, eds, *Cambridge History of Science, Vol. 7: The Modern Social Sciences* (2003), 89.
74 Hence Adshead's evidence to the 1852–3 Select Committee on Education in Manchester and Salford included information gleaned from sets of 100 Sunday scholars chosen at random from ten schools, and information from workers at a selection of factories.
75 T. Gilfoyle, *The City of Eros* (1992), 155, cited Robert Dowling, *Slumming in New York: From the Waterfront to Mythic Harlem* (2007), 4.
76 For a notion of effacement see Walkowitz, *City of Dreadful Delight*, 27.
77 Kay-Shuttleworth, *Moral and Physical*, 11.
78 See the discussion in Karen Jones and K. Williamson, 'The Birth of the Schoolroom', *Ideology and Consciousness* 6 (1979), 59–110, especially 78–83. Edmund Lyon, 'Sketch of the Medical Topography and Statistics of Manchester', *North of England Medical and Surgical Journal* I (1830–1), 1–25, 133–48. This is not to say that there are not plenty of examples of more undifferentiated discussion, such as W.B. Neale, *Juvenile Delinquency in Manchester: Its Causes and History* (1840). For a useful discussion of the specificity of place that comes from topographic mapping and the 'nomothetic thinking' that comes from

thematic mapping, see Denis Cosgrove, *Geography & Vision: Seeing, Imagining and Representing the World* (2008), 163.

79 We can see this in the Manchester material of the 'Report of the General Board of Health on the Epidemic Cholera of 1848 and 1849', *PP* (1850), 87–100.

80 See for example, F. Driver, 'Moral Geographies: Social Science and the Urban Environment in Mid-Nineteenth Century England', *Transactions of the Institute of British Geographers* ns 13 (1988), 275–87, John V. Pickstone, 'Dearth, Dirt and Fever Epidemics: Rewriting the History of British "Public Health", 1750–1850', in Terence Ranger, ed., *Epidemics and Ideas: Essays on the Historical Perception of Pestilence* (1992), 125–48.

81 R. Fishman, *Bourgeois Utopias: The Rise and Fall of Suburbia* (1987), 73–102; Anna Davin, *Growing Up Poor. School and Street in London, 1870–1914* (1996), 29–38.

82 *Manchester Spectator* (hereafter *MSp*), 17 January 1857; see *MG*, 23 January 1857; compare with comments on lack of use of parks, *MG*, 2 February 1860.

83 J.E. Mercer, *The Conditions of Life in Angel Meadow* (1897), 168–9; likewise his lament in the case of recreational provision was that 'Angel Meadow is completely forgotten', 171.

84 Brotherton letter, *MG*, 4 February 1864.

85 Royal Commission on Vaccination, Appendix VIII, *PP* (1897), 67ff.

86 See for example the case of one of the Manchester relieving officers, W.G. Clapperton, who was suspended and forced to resign after being discovered living primarily out of his district, renting a room in which he occasionally slept to try to keep up the appearance of maintaining his residence within the district, Manchester Poor Law files (1878), MH12/6068/93, 213, NA. Later cases suggest some dilution of this imperative by the mid-1880s, see the case of Thomas Price, medical officer of the second district, whose residence just beyond the boundaries of his district was sanctioned in 1885, see G. Macdonald to Local Government Board, 19 September 1885, MH12/6077/232, NA. This imperative was not confined to Poor Law; it was the first requirement of the working-class visitors of the Ladies Public Health Society that they lived in their district, see Davies, 'Health Visitor', 43.

87 A point also made in David Ward, *Poverty, Ethnicity, and the American City, 1840–1925: Changing Conceptions of the Slum and the Ghetto* (1989), 43.

88 *MCMAR* (1838), 8.

89 For a good sense of this variability, see *MCMAR* (1846), 15–25. For a descriptive report of a named district (Watson Street), see *MCMMag* (February 1849), 4–8. By 1853, the *MCMMag* was largely formally anonymising districts.

3 The cartographic imaginary

Cartography

It is doubtful, despite the arguments presented in studies such as Patrick Joyce's *Rule of Freedom*, that developments in cartography during the 30s and 40s effectively countered the tendencies towards spatial differentiation produced by organisational pressures. While the comprehensive large-scale Ordnance Survey (OS) mapping of the mid-1840s (repeated from the 1890s) might potentially have encouraged abstract understandings which, in Joyce's terms, 'homogenised space, substituting [it] for … lived, particularised positionality', the view that this regard became in any sense hegemonic seems unsustainable. The usage of maps suggests that, for all their detail and proffered panopticism, they did not deliver *power* over the city, or any sense that its spaces had been effectively controlled or neutralised.[1]

Indeed, the nature of the mapping activities of Victorian Manchester and their uses suggests the opposite. Take sanitary mapping, from the cholera maps of the 1830s and 1840s, the township surveys of the General Board of Health of the early 1850s, the comprehensive series of enumeration district maps, which John Leigh, the MOH published around 1880, and finally the survey produced by T.R. Marr in 1904. The complex histories and contexts of these maps have very recently been explored in detail in a full consideration of the history of Manchester's mapping;[2] here, I want merely to point to three features. First, the extent to which the transition from the essentially event-based map of Gaulter in 1833 to the tracing of *districts* or regions visible in the cholera and sanitary maps of the later 1840s was rarely about the construction of zonal typologies of the city. There are a few examples of zonal mapping across the period, including a three-zone sanitary map produced by John Leigh in the mid-1870s, and a two-zone map of the effect of smoke pollution on Manchester presented to the Select Committee on Smoke Prevention in 1843, and even fewer literary renditions of this sort of zonality before the 1880s.[3] Leigh and Gardiner 1849 cholera map, and the various maps produced to accompany the local inquiries of the General Board of Health between 1848 and 1854, followed by the mapping of Manchester's late-Victorian Medical Officers of Health, were all designed to demonstrate the correlation of the city's 'housing black spots' with the greatest morbidity and highest death rates.[4] This mapping was not about homogenisation, but differentiation: the more minutely the city was examined, the more variegated it came to be represented. Mapping generally focused on small districts, and although these were usually presented as not untypical specimens, detailed discussion of this sort inevitably dwelt on particularities, sustaining a sense of the city as a chequerboard of distinctive districts.[5] John Leigh's 'First Report of the Officer of Health' of 1883–1884, exemplifies this sort of verbal cartography, in the way that it offers a detailed account of particular districts, including their boundary streets, the commercial centre, the warehouse and workshop districts, the inner working-class residential districts and the outer suburbs. Leigh offers some broad sense of a diagrammatic zonal structure, red central core, yellow inner ring and blue outer ring, but carefully overlain with detailed designations of specific districts.[6] Arthur Ransome in the 1880s was still looking for the creation of detailed event-based narrative maps of disease progression and dispersal.[7]

Secondly, the way in which the maps focused ever more closely on the particular configurations of the *housing* stock of the city. During the 1870s and 1880s, John Leigh as Manchester's first MOH devoted considerable energies to a comprehensive and accurate mapping of the housing stock of the city. By the mid-1870s, he was publishing maps showing a typical concentric structure comprising the largely commercial central zone with some limited pre-1831 housing, surrounded especially in Ancoats but also in parts of other districts adjacent to Manchester township by a ring of more residential areas whose housing stock also dated to before 1831, and then a further concentric ring of those houses erected later, which he associated with artisans, clerks and those with moderate wages.[8] Not content with these, from 1879 to 1880, Leigh undertook a minute survey of the built environment of each of the sanitary districts of the three registration sub-districts which made up the Manchester township itself, publishing the maps in successive annual reports from 1881 to 1887 (see Figure 3.1).[9] The sanitary activist John Thresh, as a result of his close analysis of one sub-district of Ancoats noted that in one block, there were no less than 'twelve different lots of property easily recognisable'.[10] Leigh's sanitary maps helped to historicise the terrain of the city, and they were followed in 1904 by a further, more extensive mapping undertaken for T.R. Marr's *Housing Conditions in Manchester and Salford* (1904) (see Figure 3.2). To this extent, far from rendering space as flat and geometric, these maps sought

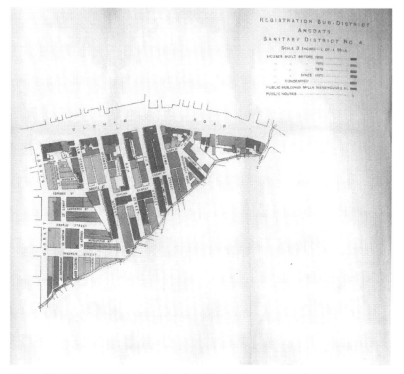

Figure 3.1 John Leigh, Registration Sub-District Ancoats, Sanitary District no. 1, from *Manchester City Council Proceedings* (1883–4), facing page 342.

to construct a complexly configured material topography, a landscape or terrain determined by the built-form of the city.[11] This was, of course, a feature of Engels' account of the city; but more pervasively we can see it in the dominant designs of city maps, especially before the 1880s, which rather than offering a transparent street grid, presented the pattern of the built environment, especially housing (Figure 3.3).

And thirdly, the relatively marginal position occupied by mapping in social debate in Victorian Manchester. It is, of course, notoriously difficult to get a secure sense of the ways maps were actually used historically, something which has undoubtedly contributed to assumptions of their 'ontic security'.[12] Maps certainly proliferated from the 1830s. Town plans, Ordnance Survey maps and other larger-scale maps, such as Adshead's 1851 map, were produced at intervals through the period. Surviving copies show how these plans were adapted to allow organisations to demonstrate the scope

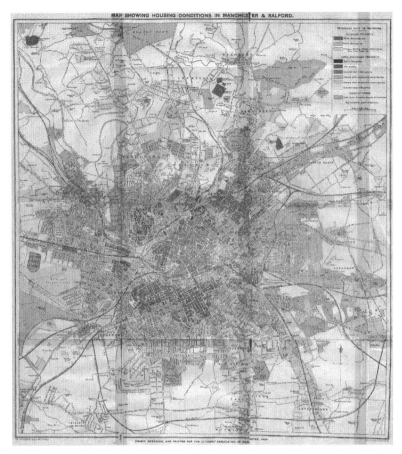

Figure 3.2 Map showing housing conditions in Manchester and Salford, from T.R. Marr, *Housing Conditions in Manchester and Salford* (1904).

of their operations, or the divisions into which their work was divided. Of course, maps were used as tools of social knowledge in the ensuing years, often indeed in the service of visiting activities. Despite the cost of such maps, there seems to have been little inhibition about annotating, marking or even, on occasion, cutting them up to create working documents to demonstrate the divisions into which their work was divided. One of the early actions of the District Provident Society was the printing of large-scale maps for distribution to visitors to 'exhibit every house and cellar'.[13] The coloured map showing coverage of operations was a fairly common staple of visiting philanthropy as much as of the local government. The coloured

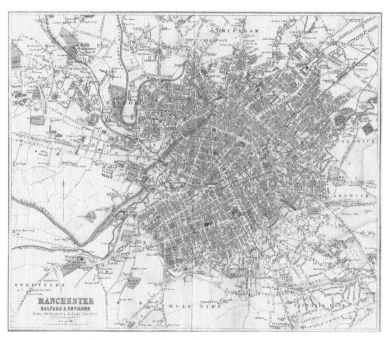

Figure 3.3 Bartholomew's map of Manchester and Salford, c. 1862.

version of a Manchester plan provided to the Poor Law Board to indicate the internal divisions of the Manchester Union has its echoes in the coloured district maps used by the M&SSA.[14] Slum clearance schemes were generating localised plans, and some were even reproduced in the local press, in the final years of the century. Around 1890, Tatham introduced the practice of depositing in each of the branch free libraries in Manchester a general health return and also weekly spot maps of diseases, showing the boundaries of the registration sub-districts and sanitary districts of Manchester, and of every infectious attack reported in the previous week, different coloured dots representing the different notifiable diseases.[15]

But even allowing for this scattered evidence of the use of maps, it seems there were astonishingly few attempts to cartographically render the social conditions of the city. Although the publication of Adshead's map was associated with a certain amount of public excitement at the level of detail it offered (a display of the whole map, stitched together and mounted on a frame, was exhibited in the mayor's parlour to crowds of several thousands[16]), maps of the city did not feature in social and political discourse in the same way that, for example, large-scale maps of the Holy Land or of empire came to be a common feature of religious lectures or missionary meetings.[17] Richard Dennis has noted how hard it is to find maps of even basic divisions such as census districts.[18] John Hatton's sanitary survey of Chorlton-upon-Medlock was presented as a lecture illustrated with a map, but when it was published in pamphlet form, the *Manchester Times* while welcoming the map, thought the list of streets with mortality rates was the most useful portion.[19] Leigh's highly suggestive housing maps were left languishing in a series of his annual reports as Medical Officer of Health, unremarked and unexploited.[20] While this mapping might potentially have encouraged greater confidence that the city was defined, divided and more amenable to access, the view that this produced the effective establishment of surveillance and hence of power seems impossible to sustain.

It was not that social questions were not conceived of spatially. It may therefore be that mapping itself was by-passed precisely because of the way, as J.B. Harley puts it, that 'maps as an impersonal type of knowledge tend to "desocialize" the territory they represent [and] foster the notion of a socially empty space'.[21] Victorian social reformers and investigators required a form that would effect the opposite, would enable them to realise socially dense and variegated space, and perhaps in part for this reason, they eschewed cartography and embraced instead what we might call a 'cartographic imaginary'.

The cartographic imaginary

Inevitably, geographical theory has engaged on a number of levels with issues implicated in the notion of a 'cartographic imaginary', but not generally in ways which adequately develop the sense in which I seek to use the term, the interrelated textual strategies and geographic images and understandings that they created.[22] Nineteenth-century cultural geography has been fascinated with fantasies of urban order, with forms of situated subjectivity or with the constitution of and conflict over behaviour in specific spaces. There has been a tendency to perceive the impulse of such practices as primarily ones of surveillance and domination, rather than of managing ignorance and impotence. Here, I am more interested in the sort of 'imaginative landscape' conjured by Judith Walkowitz, the ways in which contemporaries created mental maps of the city as a whole, which sought to bring into relationship, if not always to integrate, a number of components: the built environment, demographies (especially of class and ethnicity), a distributed framework of institutions and activities and of moral regions.[23] There is a schematic element to this process which makes it akin to notions of 'diagramming' as deployed by Osborne and Rose.[24] It also emerged out of complex relationships between rhetorical and rooted toponymies with uneven ties to any formal geographical structures, in that although some of the city's districts had precise definitions as units of ecclesiastical or local government, for example wards or registration districts, in general, understandings of the city were composed of a jigsaw of essentially rhetorical or connotative places: 'Deansgate', 'Little Ireland', 'Angel Meadow'.[25]

This was only very partially either a comprehensive or a systematic view: the cartographic imaginary of Victorian Manchester, for example, showed relatively little interest in suburban districts (except where demographic expansion created new social problems), or indeed with the central business district outside those areas of recreational significance which acquired a particular notoriety. There was a sense of occlusion emphasised by the elliptical nature of these constructions – the attempt to bring certain locales and neighbourhoods into sharp focus, while showing little interest in the intervening spaces or districts.[26] The cartographic imaginary did not produce a literature confident of laying all bare, of establishing an all-seeing gaze, but rather it registered the extent of what John Leigh described as 'hidden Manchester'.[27] Such imaginative mapping did not share in the 'geometric' pattern of contemporary cartography, but remained rooted in the older 'panoramic' forms in which it was the line of *sight* that determined the content,[28] in which space was always viewed from a particular perspective, most often that of the generic middle-class commentator, and which articulated complex topographies of the built environment.

There is a direct echo of the mapping created out of what I want to call cartographic imaginaries, in the disrupted perspectives and uneven focus of the style of 'bird's eye' view utilised by H.W. Brewer in his *Bird's Eye View of Manchester* which was published with the *Daily Graphic* in 1889.[29] Views of this sort were a feature of nineteenth-century representations of the city, and have often been treated as promoting 'what were often in reality chaotic, unregulated places as well-ordered civic communities'.[30] De Certeau talks of the 'scopic fantasy' of seeing the city mapped out from above, as 'the vast mass freezes under our gaze' and of 'the pleasure of looking down upon, of totalizing this vastest of human texts'.[31] Yet, the dominant effect offered by Brewer is precisely not even this fantasy of visibility or stability. The occupants of the street are frozen, but they still indicate crowdedness and not regular flows but the swirls and eddies of chaotic movement. And although patches of the city in both the foreground and middle ground are picked out precisely, they are situated in a wider field in which focus blurs and vision fails, leaving an overall effect which emphasises the failure of precision, not its achievement (Figure 3.4).

To fully understand this process requires a more detailed examination of contemporary understandings of Victorian Manchester. During the nineteenth century, the underlying physical geography of the city formed the base

Figure 3.4 H.W. Brewer, *Bird's Eye View of Manchester in 1889.*

for cartographic imaginaries.[32] As the city spread, for example, the extended valley of the River Irk which wound north-eastwards from the centre, and Medlock Valley which ran east–west to the south of the centre, became recognised locations of deteriorating housing, falling away to the river itself.[33] This physical geography was further defined by the transport structure and other elements of Victorian construction: canals and, increasingly from the 1840s, railway lines intersecting districts, whose characters, even their atmospheric conditions, were in turn shaped by the presence of warehouses, goods yards and industrial premises.[34] Accounts like the 1895 journalistic description of the maze of crowded streets dropping down towards the Irk from Rochdale Road, lined by the gaunt skeleton frames of its gasometers and hemmed in by the railway, constantly reinforced this sense of a variegated landscape.[35] On top of this sat the built environment proper: the configurations of the city's housing, workplaces, other public and commercial buildings, and the street plan which served them. Observers were all too aware of the further difficulties caused by the railway lines which dissected the city, their long viaducts acting as barriers to sight and communication, such as the way the Altrincham railway had blocked off and obscured the approaches to Gaythorn by the 1870s, or the railway lines and arches that 'narrow the view and block up and enshroud the streets' between Ardwick and Openshaw around the same date.[36]

From the 1830s onwards, accounts of the city were inextricably associated with a number of descriptive strategies which linked place and class to construct a highly spatialised understanding of the social structure. Perhaps the most pervasive of these was the sense that Manchester was a place in which class was marked by geographical dispersal, the 'local absenteeism' in Faucher's phrase, produced by successive phases of suburbanisation.[37] Equally powerful were contemporary perceptions of the distinctive configurations of social character produced by racial segregation, especially associated with the Irish enclaves such as New Town and Little Ireland identified by James P. Kay and successive commentators from the 1830s onwards,[38] but later encompassing anxieties about Jewish in-migration into districts such as Strangeways and Red Bank.[39] There were strong perceptions of marked variations in the density of the population. Despite contemporary anxieties at the fluidity and lack of domestic stability of many of the working-class inhabitants of the city, Victorian social analysis was also predicated on a belief in the viscosity of the working class, its tendency to live in the same narrowly defined districts, so that one consequence of slum clearance was to crowd the population even more densely into the houses that remained,[40] and for social life to be confined within a narrow geographic compass; rooted to a district of a few streets, with an unwillingness to travel beyond even for basic amenities such as education.[41] Inevitably, although it was unusual in Manchester to characterise districts on the basis of a particular occupational composition, this led to an assumption that social strata could be located geographically, and a willingness to classify areas on the basis of general social character. Although there was always a tendency of contemporary description to indulge in reductionist rhetoric which flattened all working-class districts into one mass, the picture that resulted was on the whole surprisingly discriminating. In Manchester, 'Deansgate' became well known as an area of gin places, pubs, music salons and brothels, as well as some of the oldest and most overcrowded slums.[42] Knott Mill, Gaythorn and Pin Mill Brow were recognisable as industrial ghettoes hemmed in by factories, chemical works and transport infrastructure.[43] Ancoats, the industrial heartland of the city, was itself divided into various districts: the predominantly Irish district of 'Newtown' to the north of Rochdale Road; Angel Meadow which became notorious as the lodging house quarter of the city, and so home to much of its transient if not criminal population;[44] an inner core adjacent to Great Ancoats Street, with the oldest housing and the poorest population; and then the largely undifferentiated factory district beyond.[45] The inhabitants of St George's and Ancoats registration districts were seen as primarily factory operatives, those of the Deansgate and the London Road districts as mostly railway workers, bricklayers and other semi-skilled workers. Market Street, dominated by shops and warehouses, was seen as the home of the bulk of the city's unskilled labourers, unemployed and vagrants.[46] The inner suburbs of Hulme, Chorlton and Ardwick were pictured at mid-century as being occupied by 'the class above the operative class of persons; the houses are more occupied by warehouseman and clerks'.[47] But by the 1870s, new forms of descriptive journalism, set-piece exercises in social description such as the *Manchester City News* series 'Round About Manchester' in 1871–2, were also furnishing a sense of the character of intermediate districts, and of the new industrial suburbs such as Gorton and Beswick, previously middle-class suburbs being swamped by the speculative builder such as Greenheys, and new districts of working-class housing such as Moss Side.[48] Although the precise social character of all the districts gradually changed in response to forces such as the expansion of the central business district and the shift in Manchester's economy from manufacture to commerce,[49] the social perceptions established in the early Victorian period were relatively stable. However, by the 1880s and 1890s, descriptions of some of the better working-class districts at mid-century presented their social character as having markedly deteriorated.[50]

Throughout the period, social description was fired through with a sense of massive disparities in circumstance and condition across the city, often taking the form of a rhetoric of 'holes' in the social fabric. We see this in the religious rhetoric surrounding church extension campaigns, in the debates over educational provision from at least the mid-1840s, in discussions of sanitary provision and frequently in the tendency of ward councillors to highlight the extent of 'neglect' of their wards. When, in 1840, Canon Hugh Stowell drew the attention of a Manchester Church Extension meeting to the 'vast tract between St George's-rd and St Michaels church, [where] we shall scarce find a church or a chapel of any kind', he was already drawing on a familiar concern, and one which was intensified by the debates over educational provision in the 1840s and 1850s.[51] The promotion of reforming campaigns such as the ragged school movement involved explicit claims to be tackling essentially spatial problems, providing for the worst, most neglected areas of the city.[52] The precise delineation of these localities through the tracing of boundary streets provided specificity and perhaps a reassurance of the localisation of problems, and of some containment of the potential for contagion, while at the same time effectively heightening the sense of these localities as black holes, opaque to outside view.[53]

This social topography was not inert. The division of the city into distinct districts and communities involved more than simple social description. For observers, the spatial articulation of class created complex often highly localised ecosystems of the sort described by Robert Roberts in *The Classic Slum*, social solidarities that acted powerfully to disrupt the processes of law and order and the spread of 'civilisation'. For much of the period, accounts suggested that such disruption was increasing rather than decreasing.[54] Rev. Charles Burton's account of the contrast between his reception when visiting his All Saints' parish in 1835 and again in the early 1850s, dramatised a more general feeling that by mid-century things had got considerably worse even since the 1830s. His reception in 1835, among all denominations, was presented as one of kindness, gratitude and respect with only 'five or six exceptions'; 20 years later, he reported that the inhabitants along the Medlock had entirely changed – 'a class more ignorant, filthy and depraved can nowhere be found', he told his audience, the children who 'infest' the street are 'idle, vagabonds, and vicious in the extreme'; he was pelted in Little Ireland, and his district visitors had 'been obliged entirely to abandon' a third 'of the sections in which they had previously paid their weekly calls'.[55] Although solidarities like these were initially associated especially with Irish enclaves, accounts of assaults on missionaries preaching in the open air, of the stoning of enumerators attempting to survey the use of public houses in the 1850s,[56] or of the violent resistance that the ragged school movement of the 1860s often met during its moves into a new district,[57] of 'Ancoats rowdies' in the 1870s,[58] and fiercely territorial scuttling gangs of the 1880s and 1890s,[59] all encouraged a conceptualisation of the city as constituting a social terrain powerfully resistant to the free circulation of either authority or information.

Ultimately, the built environment, social segregation and neighbourhood solidarities all served to obscure vision, to preclude or prevent the possibilities and distort the nature of social observation. This was exacerbated by the convoluted layout of the older districts, the narrow winding streets, closed courts and, in places, the warren of covered passages and small yards which led to houses further and further away from the main thoroughfares.[60]

> 'Who can master the many alleys, and courts and yards, where the stream of population does not pass, where the public eye does not rest, where human misery is never ventilated, and where the waifs and strays of humanity are eddied in, and stagnate, and fester, and pollute the air?',

as one clerical immigrant to Manchester asked in 1860.[61] The way in which the built environment of the city had evolved so as to throw up barriers to seeing, if not knowing, was of course one of the fundamental insights of Engels' account of the city in 1844, and although Engels' description, unpublished in English until the 1890s, seems to have had little direct influence on Victorian understandings, the contrast between what the *Manchester Guardian* described in 1871 as the 'thin crust of respectability' of the main thoroughfares and conditions in the interior was commonplace.[62]

Reliance on visiting encouraged such conceptions. The visiting mode was championed as the only means by which many social facts could be observed, recorded and publicised, as in the description of the Red Bank district in the early 1870s: 'No policeman ever ventured into it alone, and the City Missionary saw there scenes of horror, cruelty, outrage and vice, seldom witnessed by any other eye but God's'.[63] Because visiting organisations were not comprehensive and tended to focus on the areas of greatest need, such solidarities encouraged the tendency of social description to concentrate on a few particularly notorious areas, at times relatively detached from their place in the overall urban system.[64] In this sense, visiting created a knowledge less invested in the interrelations of different locations and their inhabitants, in, for example, modes and practices of movement across the city, than in the internal characteristics and dynamics of locality. There was an underlying anxiety about contagion and spread; however, this was powerfully checked by the focus on discrete areas, often both defined and rhetorically contained by their circumferential streets or physical features.

Ultimately this involved a recognition of the ways in which the configurations of the housing stock produced microcosmic social variations which often served to obscure vision. Leigh noted of Ancoats that it had 'not a single road or street enabling the vast population to communicate in a fairly straight line with the city with which its business chiefly lies. A series of zig-zags, along narrow streets, form its avenues to the city'.[65] The tropes of labyrinth, blind alley, dead-end courts, common in descriptions of London were equally a feature of descriptions of Manchester.[66]

Housing: Narrativising the cartographic imaginary

It was a small and common step from concerns with the configurations of housing to attention to the houses themselves. Housing was by far the most important preoccupation of social reformers from the 1840s through to the 1890s. Prior to this, there was a tendency to concentrate on the state of the street, but the reduction in the number of unpaved and unsewered streets, and the deterioration in the housing stock shifted the focus.[67] The result was what Walkowitz described as a 'complicated but well-established moral and visual semiotics' of the sort used by Booth to identify streets as rough or respectable.[68] Repeatedly, discussions with little apparent connection gravitated apparently inexorably to housing. It was not merely, as Marr put it in 1904, that 'The housing question cannot be separated from the rest of the social problem',[69] but that the social problem became indistinguishable from the question of housing.

There were a number of reasons for this preoccupation, beyond its resonance with the cultural significance accorded to the 'domestic' in the period. There was the recognition that housing type correlated strongly with crude death rates. Often, this was derived from fairly direct equations of housing age and social status, the result of what Leigh described as the 'constant tendency on the part of the more respectable artisans to leave the older parts of the city and to seek the nearer suburbs, so that gradually the old houses become filled with the poorest of the population'.[70] So John Watts' survey of St Michael's noted that the older housing stock constituted 'one of the poorest and most ignorant districts of the Borough', while the newer tenements housed 'well-paid artisans' or the 'middle class'.[71] Not least of the reasons was the way the visiting mode encouraged belief in the importance of housing as a key environmental determinant of behaviour, and its consequent capacity to create broad district typologies around a correlation between house and the social character it inscribed.[72] For Edwin Chadwick, the 'habits' of the occupiers of 'inferior tenements ... soon become "of a piece" with the dwelling'.[73] While for the journalist Angus Reach, as he put it in a well-known passage:

'Nothing struck me more, while visiting and comparing notes in the different operative districts of Manchester, than the regularity with which the better style of house and the better style of furniture went together ... A very fair proportion of what was deal in Ancoats was mahogany in Hulme. Yet the people of Hulme get no better wages than the people of Ancoats. The secret is they live in better-built houses and consequently take more pleasure and pride in their dwellings'.[74]

A culture driven by the imperative to moral differentiation between deserving and undeserving required a classification regime which facilitated less synchronic categorisation than synoptic judgement, evaluation not just of the material circumstances of a family, but also their character and deserts. Throughout the period, from the forming of the District Provident Society and the passing of the New Poor Law to the movement for organised charity or provident dispensaries, social provision in the Victorian city required an investigatory regime by which effective judgement could be made not just about the material circumstances of a family, but also about their character and deserts. Visiting offered the promise of just such a regime. Behaviour, dress and above all possessions and the condition of homes could be read for signs not just of the present situation but past conduct. 'But is it all true?', asks the narrator of one of the *Tales of Manchester Life. By a Manchester Minister* (nd, c.1870s), 'How often has this question been asked about religious tales? The editor guarantees the absolute truth of what he writes; he can take you to the house'.[75]

In theory, regular domestic visitation held out the possibility of gradually accumulating detailed case histories of the families visited. Unfortunately, as the Charity Organisation Society emphasised from the 1870s onwards, the effective construction of case histories required a degree of systematisation and regularity beyond the reach of most visiting organisations, voluntary or governmental, especially given the residential instability that marked the poorer classes.

The advantage of reading houses was that they offered the prospect of short-circuiting the laborious building up of case histories, providing a text from which observers could construct narratives, architectural and biographical, creating a knowledge which far from banishing time, sought instead to place it at the centre of things, offering evidence not merely of conditions, but also of merit.[76] Just as (as many commentators have noted) we are encouraged to read the character of the Bartons from the description of their home given at the opening of chapter 2 in *Mary Barton*. As one educational reformer put it in 1853: 'poverty and neglect of instruction go hand in hand; and …I think I could walk from street to street, and point out the houses from which children are sent to School, and those from which they are not'.[77] Houses, 'old and sodden with the filth of generations', as one sanitary reformer put it in 1890, inscribed the history of their inhabitants and enabled character to be determined.[78] In the visiting mode, to collapse Lefebvre's distinction: houses became monuments. Into the 1890s, this mode encouraged an emphasis on dirt rather than overcrowding.[79] Homologies between houses and their inhabitants, as in the 'dingy streets, swarming with dingy people' at the centre of the *Freelance*'s description of the Knott Mill district in 1875, were taken almost as axiomatic.[80] John Leigh's mapping of Ancoats' housing stock by period of construction (and indeed Marr's 1904 housing map) could thus provide, as one contemporary put it, 'a kind of chromo-chronology of the seed plots of disease in certain parts of the city'.[81]

It is this that makes sense of that facility with which Victorian social description generated social classifications read from residential standing. It was a small step from distinctions between 'the casual lodger class', taken to encompass not just 'the most fickle and ill-paid kind of labour, but the criminal and the whole debris of our social structure', the group 'represented by the worst paid forms of unskilled labour', 'casual day labourers, earning 10-20/- per week, the lower grades of which are found in sub-let cottage rooms' and the 'better positioned occupying two-roomed (usually back to back) cottages',[82] to broad social hierarchies derived from residential location, as in the fears expressed of Russell's reform bill of 1860 by one Manchester resident that

> 'the inhabitants of all the principal and more respectable streets, and of the innumerable good houses in the suburbs and neighbourhood ... the professions, merchants, masters, shopkeepers and best of the working classes ... are to be swamped by the inhabitant [sic] of back streets, courts and wretched quarters, the less respectable and least intelligent part of the community'.[83]

This front street *versus* back street opposition indicates how housing-derived social categories generated spatially intricate understandings of the urban social structure. But ultimately, equally significant was the recognition by contemporaries that all districts possessed a social mix which allowed dramatic contrasts and juxtapositions, and hence the importance of relating social position not so much to housing *type* or *location* as to housing *condition*. After all, it was the very possibility of encountering, as one of the journalists of the *Manchester City News* did in 1893, 'two houses side by side, alike as to their builder's intention; one with an unwashed door step, and a crooked-blinded air of having been drunk last night; the other clean-windowed, with cheerful red curtains', which allowed the house to symbolise the characters of their occupants.[84] As Alexander McDougall, long-time Manchester Poor Law guardian put it in 1891,

> 'The most wretched streets, the darkest courts, and most crowded dwellings have in them some of the most decent and law-abiding women and men the country possesses. They are mingled with the dissolute and depraved, retaining honesty and uprightness in the midst of profligacy and vice ...'.[85]

The shift from the preoccupation with the interior spaces, furnishings and decorations of the early Victorian house to the street by street typologies based on the external appearance of houses developed in Booth's surveys of late-Victorian London was belated and slow.[86]

The durability of the visiting mode derived in part from its particular suitability for the creation of this sort of knowledge, from its, as one Statistical Society survey of the 1860s put it, 'prosecut[ion] ... from house to house'.[87] Understanding did not proceed, as Poovey suggests, via extrapolation, but rather through cases rooted in specific sites. Contemporaries did not conceive of class structure as comprising groups of abstracted individuals, but as situated social trajectories.

Notes

1 Joyce, *Rule of Freedom*, 36.
2 For a general study, see Terry Wyke, Brian Robson, Martin Dodge, *Manchester: Mapping the City* (2018).
3 *Select Committee on Smoke Prevention*, PP (1843), VII, Q868-71; though note the concentric construction provided by *Bradshaw's Illustrated Guide to Manchester* (1857), as cited in Fishman, *Bourgeois Utopias*, 75–6. One indication of the shift is the discussion of zones in the 'General Report for the Year 1879 by Her Majesty's Inspector H.E. Oakeley ... on Schools Inspected by Him in the Manchester District', *PP* (1880), XXII, 386–402, or for example McDougall's evidence to *PP* (1895), Q5157-60; *PP* (1895), XIV, 401. (In passing, the same could be said for cartographic descriptions: even in those cases, for example the descriptions of Angus Reach, C. Aspin, ed., *Manchester and the Textile Districts in 1849* (1972), where we do get some approach to a zoned description of the city, the emphasis remains firmly on complexity within the zones, especially in respect of working-class housing.)
4 See also Leigh's mapping of mortality rates by census enumeration district, *MCCP* (1873–4), and his mapping of the different ages of housing stock in his *Medical Officer of Health's Report for 1876* (see 614.0942 M4, Manchester Archives).
5 One good example of this, with its detailed maps, is A. Ransome, 'Where Consumption is Bred in Manchester and Salford', *Health Journal* (November 1887), 88–90. For the way in which this contrasts with other European practices, see Marjaana Niemi, 'Public Health Discourses in Birmingham and Gothenburg, 1890–1920', in S. Sheard and H. Power, eds, *Body and City: Histories of Urban Public Health* (2000), 123–42.
6 Medical Officer of Health's 'Annual Report', *MCCP* (1883–4), 308–13.
7 See Arthur Ransome, 'On the Need for a Systematic Study of Epidemic Disease', *BMJ*, 27 August 1881, 353–4.
8 Medical Officer of Health's *Annual Report for 1875–6*, 280–1; compare with the similar mapping in Medical Officer of Health's 'Annual Report', *MCCP* (1883–4), 308–13.
9 That is, the original township, not including the separate townships of Hulme and Chorlton that had been joined to Manchester when it was incorporated at the start of the Victorian period.
10 Thresh, *Enquiry*, 10.

11 For distinction, see for example, Driver, 'Moral Geographies', 277–8.

12 Pamela K. Gilbert, 'The Victorian Social Body and Urban Cartography', in *idem*, ed., *Imagined Londons* (2002), 11–30. For information on the use made of maps by another clerical/missionary investigator, Abraham Hume of Liverpool, see Bosworth, 'Hume', 61.

13 *Manchester Times*, 6 July 1833, *MG*, 27 July 1833. In a similar way, John Watts noted his management of the National Public Schools Association (NPSA) statistical survey of St Michael's and St John's involved preparation from the Ordnance Survey (OS) map of a 'Street and Court List' by which investigation was divided up among canvassers, John Watts, *Report upon the Statistical Inquiry ... in St Michael's and St John's Wards, in November and December 1852* (1853), 1. The 1856 Sunday School canvass used both a 6 inch to the mile OS map and a 60 inches to the mile map which was cut up into the 20 districts into which the city had been divided, *MX*, 2 August 1856.

14 MH12/6044/106-10, NA; or the M&SSA map of districts, M126/3/1-2.

15 *MCN*, 25 April 1891. In the 1880s, both the Manchester and Salford Sick Poor and Private Nursing Institution and the Ladies Sanitary Association were providing colour-coded maps showing the districts in which they operated in their *Annual Reports*, see Scott, 'The Need for Better Organisation of Benevolent Effort in Manchester and Salford', 148; or James Niven giving details of unwholesome house clearance to the North West Branch of the Incorporated Society of Medical Officers of Health, with various maps and plans showing the districts involved, *Public Health* 16 (1893–4), 393–6; this material was also gradually making an appearance in the press by the 1890s, see 'The Condemned Slums in Salford', *Manchester Weekly Times*, 7 November 1890. For examples of the micro-district plans, see the 'Report as to Unhealthy Dwellings', *MCCP* (1886–7), 120–32, which contained a number of examples of especially enclosed housing blocks, including Nadin's Court off Silk Street, approached by two covered passages, one 3 foot 6 inches wide, and the other a foot narrower.

16 *Manchester Times*, 3 November 1849, 23 August 1851; it was described as more effective than the OS maps because of its colour, and was likened to Wyld's Globe, a contemporary London attraction. Note the parallel with Booth's public display of large-scale versions of his poverty maps of settlement houses in the 1890s. C. Topalov, 'The City as Terra Incognita: Charles Booth's Poverty Survey and the People of London, 1886–1891', *Planning Perspectives* 8 (1993), 418.

17 See Felix Driver, *Geography Militant. Cultures of Exploration and Empire* (2001), 79–80.

18 R. Dennis, *Cities in Modernity* (2008), 66.

19 John Hatton, *A Lecture on the Sanitary Condition of Chorlton upon Medlock* (1854); *MX*, 14 January 1854. For another similar use, see reference to the map of parts of Hulme showing cholera, used in an M&SSA lecture, *MX*, 19 November 1853.

20 Marr, *Housing*, 3, on the lack of influence of Leigh's MOH reports; compare with *Health Journal* IV (1886–7), 33. (Though they were quoted extensively by Robert Blatchford in his 'Modern Athens' series in the *Sunday Chronicle* in 1889.)

21 J.B. Harley, 'Maps, Knowledge and Power', in Denis Cosgrove and Stephen Daniels, *The Iconography of Landscape* (1988), 277–312, quote at 303.

22 Standard accounts include Kevin Lynch, *The Image of the City* (1960).

23 This is visible also in the idea of 'common-sense' maps deployed by Barry M. Doyle, 'Mapping Slums in a Historic City: Representing Working Class Communities in Edwardian Norwich', *Planning Perspectives* 16 (2001), 47–65. For a suggestive consideration of a component of the metropolitan imaginary, see Pamela K. Gilbert, '"Scarcely to Be Described": Urban Extremes as Real Spaces and Mythic Places in the London Cholera Epidemic of 1854', *Nineteenth Century Studies* 14 (2000), 149–72. The notion of moral regions was established by Robert Park in his essay 'The city: suggestions for the investigation of human behaviour' (1915), see *idem*, *The City* (1925).

24 '[A]n activity of thought that is as much technical as cognitive; not a literal diagram but an abstraction, something more akin to a model, but not a model but an "operative rationale" which projects a certain "truth" about the city; "virtual maps, maps of the codes immanent in forces and their relations"'. T. Osborne and N. Rose, 'Governing Cities: Notes on the Spatialisation of Virtue', *Environment and Planning D: Society and Space* 17 (1999), 737–60, 739.

25 See William Sharpe and Leonard Wallock, 'From "Great Town" to "Nonplace Urban Realm": Reading the Modern City', in Sharpe and Wallock, eds, *Visions of the Modern City: Essays in History, Art and Literature* (1987), 17.

26 For this process of conceptual asyndeton, see the discussion in Michel de Certeau, *The Practices of Everyday Life. Volume 1* (1984), 101–2.

27 Leigh, 'Annual Report', *MCCP* (1869–70), 115.

28 Louis Marin, *Utopics. The Semiological Play of Textual Spaces* (1984), cited in Nead, *Victorian Babylon*, 21.

29 See Brewer's *Bird's Eye View of Manchester* (1889), published with the *Daily Graphic*. There are numerous examples of this variegated field, see Waters, *Sanitary Condition of Manchester*, which concentrates on the worst areas.

30 Cosgrove, *Geography and Vision*, 178, citing John W. Reps, *Views and Viewmakers of Urban America: Lithographs of Towns and Cities in the United States and Canada, 1825–1925* (1984), Alison Byerly, '"A Prodigious Map Beneath His Feet": Virtual Travel and The Panoramic Perspective', *Nineteenth-Century Contexts* 29.2 (2007), 151–68.

31 Michel de Certeau 'Walking in the City', reprinted in Graham Ward, ed., *The Certeau Reader* (2000), 101, quoted in Ruth Livesey, 'Women Rent Collectors and the Rewriting of Space, Class and Gender in East London, 1870–1900', in Elizabeth Darling, Lesley Whitworth, eds, *Women and the Making of Built Space in England, 1870–1950* (2007), 87–105.

32 A line of argument consistent with ideas of the 'formal logic' which space creates that have been developed in writings on 'space syntax'; see 'The Spatial Syntax of Urban Segregation', special edition of *Progress and Planning* 67.3 (2007).

33 See, for example, *MCN*, 11 June 1870. Thomas Southwood Smith and P.H. Holland, 'Inquiry into the Sanitary Condition of the Inhabitants Resident on the Banks of the Rivers and Streams Flowing into and through Manchester', *Royal Commission into the Sewage of Towns, Second Report, PP* (1861) XXXIII, 44–8.

34 For contemporary recognition of the impact of the railways on the city see J.R. Kellet, *The Impact of Railways on the Victorian City* (1969); Brian Rosa, 'Beneath the Arches: Re-appropriating the Spaces of Infrastructure in Manchester', unpublished PhD, University of Manchester (2014).

35 See 'A Looker On: Sidelights on Local Election Work', *MCN*, 13 July 1895.

36 *MG*, 13 April 1871, 'Round About Manchester', *MCN*, 7 December 1872. Compare the picture of Red Bank in B. Williams, *The Making of Manchester*

Jewry 1740–1875 (1985), 'socially barricaded by the railway and industries in the polluted valley of the Irk, and so neglected and ill-lit as to be in a state of "perpetual midnight"', 81. Laura Vaughan, 'Jewish Immigrant Settlement Patterns in Manchester and Leeds 1881', *Urban Studies* 43.3 (2006), 653–72, especially 664–5, confirms the way in which the 'axial lines' of the city's street layout helped segregate Red Bank. Likewise, Fishman notes the psychologically segregating effects of the railway lines, *East End 1888: A Year In a London Borough among the Labouring Poor* (1988), 2.

37 Faucher, *Manchester in 1844*, 26. The classic statement is perhaps Richard Parkinson, *On the Present Condition of the Labouring Poor in Manchester; with Hints for Improving It* (1841).

38 Faucher, *Manchester in 1844*, 28–9; in support, the local editor J.P. Culverwell cited Howard on Little Ireland, 'those quarters where the Irish congregate are the worst' in their sanitary condition.

39 Articles on Hightown, *MCN*, 17, 24 January 1891 and 'Rambler', *MCN*, 13 February 1892 offer just two examples of a very common construction of Jewish quarters in the 1890s. The sense of ethnic segregation, even of Jews, is visible in the accounts of Samuel Kydd to *Reynolds's Weekly News*, 9, 16 August 1857. Although there was an element of impressionistic prejudice here, M.A. Busteed, 'The Irish in Nineteenth-Century Manchester', *Irish Studies Review* 18 Spring (1997), 8–13, shows 'highly significant patterns of marked residential segregation', concentrated especially in the inner areas of Angel Meadow set well back from the main thoroughfares, 11.

40 'The poor cling to the old localities, and are thus driven to herd more and more closely together, and greatly to overcrowd the houses which remain', Ransome and Royston, *Health*, 16; and also Mercer on Angel Meadow's 'old families, long settled in the place', Mercer, *The Conditions of Life in Angel Meadow*, 162.

41 See the discussion of Stokes on the failure of St Chad's to attract children from Angel Meadow to Cheetham Hill Road and ultimately the building of a second school in Angel Meadow, S.N. Stokes, 'Report [on Catholic Schools..]', *Report of the Committee of Council on Education*, PP (1868–9), XX, 316–7.

42 See the account of St John's ward, LIBERTY, *MCN*, 19 August 1893.

43 For Knott Mill see T.R. Wilkinson, 'Report on the Educational and Other Conditions of a District at Gaythorn and Knott Mill, Manchester, Visited in January 1868, with Observations Suggested by the Visitation', *TMSS* (1867–8), 53–77; 'A Prospect from Knott Mill', *Freelance* X (1875), 218. This was a recognised 'problem' from the early Victorian period, see *MC*, 11 April 1840; *MX*, 18 August 1849, letter of GJ, *MG*, 24 February 1859. See also the recollections of the Hewitt Street Board School (previously St Peter's Ragged School), *MCN*, 6 January 1940.

44 'The Census in the Slums: Charter-Street (Angel Meadow)', *MG*, 6 April 1871, *MCN*, 3 January 1885; Mercer, *Angel Meadow*, and discussion, *MCN*, 1 May 1897.

45 The divisions of Ancoats are clear in William Royston, 'Sanitary State of Ancoats', *MX*, 15 March 1854.

46 See J. Whitehead, *The Rate of Mortality in Manchester* (1863), especially 42–52.

47 For perceptions at mid-century see the evidence of Adshead in the *Select Committee on Education in Manchester and Salford. First Report*, PP (1852) XI, Q1974.

48 'Round about Manchester' series, *MCN*, 21 October, 18 November, 2, 16 December 1871, 13, 27 January 1872; *MCN*, 25 May 1872.

49 As in the degeneration of St John's ward, furthered by limited slum clearances in Deansgate (including for the new Midland and Great Northern stations in the 1890s), and by the presence of abattoirs and the Municipal Cleansing Department yard, see letter of LIBERTY, *MCN*, 19 August 1893.

50 Examples of late century accounts include 'Manchester Sundays, by A Looker On. Number 1. In the City Road', *MCN*, 20 June 1896.

51 *MC*, 25 January 1840, 10 April 1841 (in respect of the Ten Churches Association), *MC*, 2 April 1842. See also 'Manchester Man and Manchester Manners', *North of England Magazine* (1843), 180–3.

52 For example, see the debates on adult education in Ancoats, including *MSp*, 14 February 1857, letter of JA, *MG*, 13 October 1864. This approach was characteristic of propaganda for educational provision, see St Michael's District, Angel Meadow File, National Schools Archive, Church of England Record Office.

53 We can see these as examples of what Frederic Jameson describes as 'strategies of containment', part of the attempt to isolate working-class culture in order to disable and ultimately destroy it, Jameson *The Political Unconscious. Narrative as Socially Symbolic Act* (1981). See also the argument of Nead, 'From Alleys to Courts'.

54 For an early example, see the account given by Edwin Chadwick of the problems of enforcing ejectment for non-payment of rents in 'some of the worst neighbourhoods of Manchester', Poor Law Commissioners Sanitary Inquiry, 235, quoted in David Englander, *Landlord and Tenant in Urban Britain, 1838–1918* (1983), 14.

55 The destruction of Irish properties by the construction of Oxford Road railway station led to migration across the Medlock replacing single operative households by dense overpopulation – despite increasing numbers of schools and chapels, *MX*, 15 March 1854.

56 *MX*, 8, 12, 26 July 1854. In the 1830s, it was particularly associated with ethnic enclaves, see John Roberton as reported in *MG*, 6 January 1838.

57 Naylor-street Ragged School, *MG*, 29 November 1860; Manchester and Salford Ragged School Union, *Annual Report* (1866–7); 'An Example for Young Men's Associations', *Young Men's Magazine* II (1859), 321, which talks of stones through the fanlights, dead cats and dogs thrown into the side passage. For parallel examples in London, see the account of the beginning of his mission by Rev. C.F. Lowder, *Ten Years in S. George's Mission. Being an Account of Its Origins, Progress and Works of Mercy* (1867), 6. See Mervyn Busteed, 'Little Islands of Erin: Irish Settlement and Identity in Mid-Nineteenth Century Manchester', in Donald M. MacRaild, ed., *The Great Famine and Beyond: Irish Migrants in Britain in the Nineteenth and Twentieth Centuries* (2000), 94–127.

58 *MCN*, 1 December 1866, viz *MG*, 2 May 1865, 5 November 1866, *The Sphinx* (1871), 82.

59 Andrew Davies. 'Youth Gangs, Masculinity and Violence in Late Victorian Manchester and Salford', *Journal of Social History* (1998), 349–69, *idem*, '"These Viragoes are No Less Cruel than the Lads": Young Women, Gangs and Violence in Late Victorian Manchester and Salford', *British Journal of Criminology* 39.1 (1999), 72–89. Compare accounts of earlier gang fights, for example the Little Ireland versus Charter Street fight in 1850, *MX*, 6 November 1850.

60 Report on the Sanitary Condition of Chorlton Union, *MG*, 15 November 1865. The description of Ransome and Royston, *Health of Manchester*, 7, was 'They are entered by a narrow arched passage, and closed at both ends, often by high

buildings; they are but a few yards, and sometimes feet, in breadth; they have houses on both sides varying in number from 1 to 6 and 8 or more'.

61 Manchester and Salford Sunday Ragged School Union, *Annual Report* (1860), 25.

62 'Census in the Slums: Ancoats', *MG*, 5 April 1871; compare *MG*, 15 March 1860, which comments on the 'showy tenements' of shopkeepers and tradesmen masking the wholly working-class quarters within. For another case, see Leigh, *MCCP* (1869–70), 115, compare the letter of Charles Atkinson, *MG*, 9 August 1879; memorandum of Layhe, M&SSA Papers, M126/2/1/14, Manchester Archives.

63 MacGill and Weigall, *Seeking and Saving*, 5.

64 A point also made in Ward, *Poverty, Ethnicity, and the American City*, 43.

65 Quoted Rosa, 'Beneath the Arches', 87.

66 See Yelling, *Slums*, 19–20.

67 Replies to questions of Holland in *Royal Commission on the State of Large Towns. First Report, PP* (1844), XVII, Appendix, 58–70.

68 Walkowitz, *City of Dreadful Delight*, 34.

69 Marr, *Housing*, 14.

70 John Leigh, *MOH Report* (1876). This was a consistent theme of the district sanitary reports of the 1848–54 period, see for example, Royston on Ancoats, *MX*, 15 March 1854.

71 See the case of John Watts' survey of St Michael's, which noted the older housing stock as 'one of the poorest and most ignorant districts of the Borough', but newer tenements which housed 'well-paid artisans' or the 'middle class'. Watts, *Statistical Enquiry*, 1.

72 See, for example, Gilbert, *Cholera*.

73 Chadwick, *Report on the Sanitary Condition of the Labouring Population of Great Britain in 1842*, quoted Goodlad, *Victorian State*, 93; see similar homologies in Adshead, *Distress*, 47.

74 Aspin, *Manchester and Textile Districts*, 2–4; an approach replicated in the series 'On the Social Condition of the Working Classes of Manchester', in *MX*, January–February 1852, the contrast of whose two main districts was presented as one of cleanliness, tidiness and comfort resulting from the greater 'self-respect' of the inhabitants, 4 February 1852. For an insightful discussion of some of these themes, see Goodlad, *Victorian State*, especially chapter 3.

75 *Tales of Manchester Life. By a Manchester Minister* ([1870s]), 129. Compare with the comment of James Hammack, a census commissioner, that 'The houses of a country are a sure index to the condition of its inhabitants. This is especially true with respect to the working classes, whose physical condition is greatly dependent on the state of their dwellings', Levitan, *British Census*, 107, citing *Transactions of the National Association for the Promotion of Social Science* (1859), 107.

76 For examples of this, see the article on the Ladies Sanitary Association, *MG*, 18 January 1890; letter of George Heap, *MCN*, 12 April 1890.

77 Watts, *Statistical Enquiry*, 4. 'Wherever we find a clean and comfortable cottage, it may be fairly assumed that its inmates are moral and intelligent', commented Buckland in 1840, *MTPAR* (1840), 30.

78 *The Lancet* (July–December 1890), 644. This is a distinct but not incompatible dynamic to the contrast of dilapidation and modernity identified in Mayne, *Imagined Slum*, 171–2.

79 See the results of inspections of the Ladies Sanitary Association, reported in Tatham's *Quarterly Report, MCN*, 3 March 1894.

80 'A Prospect from Knott Mill', *Freelance* X (1875), 218.

81 Crosfield, *Bitter Cry*, 14. For an interesting study of the ways in which houses continued in some sense to function in this way after 1900, see N. Hayes, '"Calculating Class": Housing, Lifestyle and Status in the Provincial English City, 1900–1950', *Urban History* 36.1 (2009), 113–40.

82 *MCN*, 28 June 1890. Note echoes here of the 'housing classes' identified by John Rex in post-1945 Birmingham, Rex, *Race, Community and Conflict* (1967), for example, 35–9: 'in the [fluid] housing economy, occupiers tend to settle in houses finely tuned to their circumstances and characters'.

83 *MG*, 15 March 1860.

84 'A Day's Round with the Sanitary Woman', *Manchester City News*, 4 November 1893.

85 Alexander McDougall, *Drink and Poverty* ([1891]), 7. See also George Rooke, 'The Cost of Administering the English Poor Law', citing Thomas Charlton to the Manchester Statistical Society in 1876, 'The greater part of the cases of out-door relief are to be found in the most densely crowded districts, living in the worst possible character of houses or dwellings. They are the poor and spiritless dregs of humanity, ill-fed, worse-clothed and very often dirty and foul...' (cited 95).

86 Walkowitz, *City of Dreadful Delight*, 34.

87 See, for example, the details of the method in Oats, 'Deansgate', 1–13.

4 The nineteenth-century visiting mode and Elizabeth Gaskell's fiction

Introduction

The domestic visit was a component of the short stories of nineteenth-century women's magazines, of religious and philanthropic periodicals, and in novels, from Austen's *Emma* to Eliot's *Middlemarch*.[1] These accounts, whether they offered the powerfully negative tone of Mrs Pardiggle's insensitive and blinkered encounters with a London bricklayer of Dickens' *Bleak House* (itself counterposed by the combination of empathy and system embodied in Esther Summerson)[2] or the transformative death-bed experience of Mary Brotherton in Frances Trollope's *Michael Armstrong, the Factory Boy* (1839–40), were repeatedly represented as knowledge transactions and potential moments of learning, and rehearsed the conventional components of the visiting mode narrative. Hence, the worldly Manchester novelist Geraldine Jewsbury was not just driven to visiting, but also to framing her mid-century novel *Marian Withers* with an opening scene involving a servant despatched to a 'back-garden street' to deliver clothes to two impoverished children, complete with a guide (the 'pawnbroker's man), threats from the 'hulking men' in the doorways, a dark and enclosed cellar dwelling, leading to the heroine's vicarious learning of the 'invisible world' of the city's outcast children.[3]

The traction of the visiting mode as a way of understanding the industrial city is particularly powerfully represented in the work of Elizabeth Gaskell. Gaskell addressed urban society primarily in her two Manchester-based condition of England novels, *Mary Barton* (1848) and *North and South* (1854–5) (where Manchester is thinly disguised as 'Milton-Northern'),[4] but also in a number of shorter stories set in Manchester, several published under the pseudonym Cotton Mather Mills in *Howitt's Journal*, including 'The Three Eras of Libbie Marsh', and others which appeared in Dickens' *Household Words*, including 'Lizzie Leigh' and 'The Manchester Marriage',[5] and in many of her non-Manchester novellas and short stories, including *Cranford*

(1851–3) (along with its prequel, *Mr Harrison's Confessions* (1851)), *Ruth* (1853) and *A Dark Night's Work* (1863).[6] Taken together, Gaskell's writing reveals the intimate exchanges of the realist novel with visiting as practice and paradigm.[7]

The story that Gaskell's inspiration for her first novel came while visiting a poor family in Manchester, when she was grabbed tightly by the father of the family, and asked 'have you ever seen a child clemmed to death?',[8] may be apocryphal, but visiting was crucial to Gaskell's writing. Her own personal experience of visiting was probably limited – the lack of any substantial reference in contemporary sources, including her own correspondence would suggest this – but she did do some prison visiting,[9] and later recollections claim that she also visited for the DPS,[10] for her class at the Lower Mosley Street Sunday School and apparently also to a district in Chorlton-upon Medlock.[11] And indirect exposure to visiting pressed on her from every side. Her husband William was prominent in the Manchester Domestic Mission and the M&SSA, and took a leading role in establishing the Unitarian Home Mission Board, many of whose students acted as visitors for the DPS.[12] Gaskell's daughters visited,[13] and her close friends included Susanna Winkworth who also acted as a visitor for the DPS in Ancoats,[14] and Travers Madge, 'a zealous amateur missionary amongst the Manch[este]r poor'.[15] Winkworth's account of a Sunday party in 1849 at which she and Madge were catechised by the historian J.A. Froude about their visiting and the needs of the poor illuminates the importance of visiting knowledge in this milieu.[16]

Gaskell recognised the role of visiting in part as the acquisition of information about social conditions.[17] She herself drew directly for key descriptions of working-class conditions and attitudes on the writings of those like the journalist Angus Reach operating in the 'visiting mode', and especially on the reports of the Manchester Domestic Mission, including short passages of very direct reproduction of the observations of John Layhe the missioner during the later 1830s and 1840s.[18] And while she was aware of the dangers of visiting literature offering formulaic and 'touched up' accounts, and maintained a clear distinction in her mind between the 'facts' which visitors could acquire and the opinions they might develop from them, in her correspondence during the 1850s and 1860s she repeatedly recommended local visitors as the most effective sources of local knowledge.[19]

Knowledge realism

Scholarship has tended to treat Gaskell's position as a realist novelist with ambivalence, along the lines of John Gross's verdict that '*Mary Barton* survives chiefly as documentary'.[20] Gaskell herself had no such qualms. Even if all else might be dismissed as worthless, she claimed at least that her work was based on fact; and she justified her intervention on the basis of her intimate knowledge of the working poor; 'those best acquainted with the way of thinking & feeling among the poor acknowledge its *truth*', she told one correspondent, of *Mary Barton*, 'which is the acknowledgement I most of all desire'.[21] Contemporary critical debate agreed that she was successful and significant precisely insofar as she was representational,[22] praising her above all as a medium of knowledge; most obviously in Charles Kingsley's much-cited litany:

> 'Do [the rich] ... want to know why poor men, kind and sympathising as women to each other ... learn to hate law and order, ...? Then let them read *Mary Barton*. Do they want to get a detailed insight into the whole "science of starving" ... Let them read Mary Barton. ... if they want to know why men ... turn sceptics, Atheists, blasphemers, ... let them read *Mary Barton*'.[23]

Knowledge was not just a pervasive theme of Gaskell's fiction, it was its overriding structural preoccupation.[24] 'Know one another, the idea impressed on every part of *North and South*', as one review put it, is established by the first real conversation between its emblematic protagonists Margaret Hale and John Thornton: 'You do not know anything about the South', Margaret protests; 'And may I say', Thornton retorts, 'you do not know the North' (*N&S*, 122–3).[25] *Mary Barton* equally is propelled by John Barton's belief that the government could not possibly know of working-class misery, by his faith that 'better times [will] come after Parliament knows all' and by his crushing disillusion when the government 'so cruelly refused to hear us' (*MB*, 130, 145). Throughout Gaskell's writing there is a general valorisation of the 'strong healthy craving after further knowledge' (*CP*, 271), visible in Ruth's craving, despite her outcast status, for learning of various sorts, or in the desire of the factory girl Bessy Higgins 'to know so many things' (*N&S*, 133). Gaskell's heroines and heroes are open to learning, her villains have closed minds.

Mary Barton and *North and South* are novels more of diagnosis than therapeutics, and criticism which focuses on the feebleness of their curative action to some extent misses the point. 'Meddling twixt master and man', as Bessy's father Nicholas Higgins tells Margaret in *North and South*, 'takes a deal o' wisdom for to do ony good' (*N&S*, 384). And wisdom (or at least knowledge) is exactly what is lacking. Just as the rich dancers are ignorant of the meaning of winter to the poor at the outset of *Ruth* (12), so the envy of the roadside workers in *A Dark Night's Work* is entirely superficial ('And yet if they had known – if the poor did know – the troubles and temptations of the rich' (48)). John Barton's tragedy was the combination of thoughtfulness and ignorance.[26] Ultimately, he is 'almost crushed with the knowledge of the consequences of his own action' (*MB*, 435). The master Carson is equally a victim of structural ignorance: the channelling of his energies into the narrow run of economic success 'prevented him from becoming largely and philosophically comprehensive in his views' (*MB*, 451); as was the son of the hard-nosed employer, Hamper, a 'young man ... half-educated as regarded information, and wholly uneducated as regarded any other responsibility than that of getting money' (*N&S*, 519).

If Gaskell offers any solution it is implicitly educational, looking to the open articulation and explanation of actions. The failing of the masters was that 'they did not choose to make all these facts known' (*MB*, 21), or felt it unnecessary to give their reasons, so that the employers became 'known only to those below them as desirous to obtain the greatest quantity of work for the lowest wages' (*MB*, 435–6). Barton and Nicholas Higgins, his counterpart in *North and South*, both articulate this failure of the middle classes to educate: 'No one learned me, and no one told me' Barton says, 'they taught me to read, and then they ne'er gave me no books' (*MB*, 440). Higgins tells Mr Hale, 'If yo', sir, or any other knowledgeable, patient man come to me, and says he'll larn me what the words mean ... why in time I may get to see the truth to it' (*N&S*, 293, viz 207 and 364).

Anti-statistical knowledge

There was little sense of state surveillance in Gaskell's fiction. Such knowledge as there is lies in the institutions of local voluntarism. The police are an occasional threat to liberty, but not a panoptic presence. They are cunning enough to trick Mrs Wilson into identifying Henry Carson's murder weapon, but generally in the dark about the murder, overlooking crucial evidence and misinterpreting what they have. They cannot lead John Barton to his sister-in-law Esther, who is easily able to evade the beat patrols.[27] The factory inspector may be wise to attempts to inflate the ages of children so as to enable them to get work in the factories, but controls on smoke pollution are nugatory, the necessary informers non-existent. Parliament, observes Thornton, is merely 'a meddler with only a smattering of knowledge of the real facts of the case' (*N&S*, 125).

Nor does Gaskell have any sympathy with modes of statistical knowledge. This antipathy is often coded as a rejection of 'theory', most famously at the outset of *Mary Barton* where Gaskell signals that she intends to operate outside the procedures of 'political economy', but it is equally visible in the way Margaret Hale is set up as the voice of one who knows nothing of political economy.[28] Theory is repeatedly opposed to the practical knowledge of everyday engagement, part of a reiterated dismissal of mere book learning. The visited poor, as worldly and ambitious Ralph Corbet observes in *A Dark Night's Work*, 'were all very well in their way; and if they could have been brought to illustrate a theory hearing about them might have been of some use' (90). But the factory hand Higgins, the industrialist Thornton and even the Oxford don Mr Bell share the same stance. '[T]he philosopher and the idiot, publican and Pharisee, all eat after the same fashion – given an equally good digestion. There's theory for theory for you', remarks Bell, while Thornton claims 'I have no theory; I hate theories'. Higgins 'prefers', as Jenny Uglow has put it, 'to speak from direct experience'.[29] The world, he observes, 'needs fettling' (*N&S*, 382).[30]

More than this, as Caroline Levine has recently pointed out, Gaskell refuses to count.[31] She might not indulge in the sledgehammer sarcasm of *Hard Times*, but she shares Dickens' suspicion of statistical thinking.[32] Her scattered references to statistics are ironical and subversive: hence the 'curious statistical fact' observed in *Mr Harrison's Confessions* that 'five-sixths of our householders of a certain rank in Duncombe are women'. Enumeration unnerved, averages were presented as alien and unhelpfully impersonal, invalidated by the social categorisation their arithmetic required.[33] Higgins recognises that the failing of the book he is given by his employer is that it speaks of people as mere abstractions ('vartues or vices'). He understands that 'truth can[not] be shaped out in words, all neat and clean, as th' men at th' foundry cut out sheet iron' (*N&S*, 292–3).[34] The collapse of the strike in *Mary Barton* arises from a failure of its leaders to understand that the men are not machines but are creatures of emotion. It is this that makes sense of Job Legh's otherwise enigmatic observation to Mr Carson, 'You can never work facts as you would fixed quantities and say, given two facts, and the product is so and so' (*MB*, 457). Carson's problem, as he comes to realise, is that he knows his men not by name as individuals, but only *en masse*, just as Thornton is brought to recognise that 'hands', though the 'technical term', dehumanises his employees (*N&S*, 166).

Gaskell is particularly severe on the reduction of individuals to economic position. She is aware of the subtle gradations of Manchester's social structure, as registered by her reference to the apparent extravagance of the diets of fine spinners in 'Libbie Marsh'. But she refuses to type people by occupation, recognising this as a strategy of psychological control, without which 'the people rise up to life', irritating and terrifying (*MB*, 220).[35] The inadequacy of judgements derived from occupational stereotypes is a running theme of *North and South*, symbolised by the Hales' dismissal of Thornton as 'tradesman',[36] just as Higgins is 'bamboozled' by Thornton's refusal to be confined by the category of 'master' and Thornton is 'taken aback' with Higgins in the same way (*N&S*, 418–19).

Here, I take issue with Emily Steinlight's recent suggestion that Gaskell's work is 'geared less toward the representation of a fixed class of "working men" than toward the making of statistical remainders'.[37] Indeed, Gaskell rejects the exclusionary impetus of the 'census mentality' which defines by occupation and construes the unemployed as an apparently indescribable residuum. People can only be known, she urges, outside the statistical categories imposed upon them, not as generalities, but as individuals.[38] This stance is given its fullest expression in the unsympathetic portrait of Richard Bradshaw in *Ruth*, in his reliance on maxims not feelings, his insistence on applying black-and-white judgements and his treatment of Ruth as a category ('sinner') rather than as an individual with a history.[39] In contrast, the response of Thurstan Benson, Ruth's protector, to the exposure of Bradshaw's wrongdoing is a refusal to identify him as 'criminal' 'without first ascertaining the particulars about him' (*Ruth*, 282).

Gaskell's characters are not just social units; they are, as Uglow points out, 'endowed with pasts'.[40] These pasts provide character, the unmeasurable measure of an individual's identity. So Jem understands his workmates' ostracism of him: they 'have nought to stand upon ... but their character' (*MB*, 430). As a result, although Gaskell continues to invoke a binary division of rich and poor, Dives and Lazarus, 'with a great gulf betwixt us' (*MB*, 45, viz 219, echoed in *N&S*, 202),[41] she is more interested in questioning undifferentiated constructions of 'the poor', against which she offers the character-based gradations of Victorian philanthropy, 'the loose-living and vicious, ... the decent poor, ... the well-to-do and respectable' (*Ruth*, 295). Uncovering these pasts is not without its challenges, but it is essential to knowing. Thornton's discovery that Higgins had waited five hours for him at the factory gate prompts him 'to going about collecting evidence as to the truth of Higgins's story', going beyond simple categories to the 'nature of his character', beyond his position to 'the tenor of his life' (*N&S*, 403).

Visiting fictions

It was this importance of history and character which established home rather than street or workplace as the fundamental site of social observation. At the start of *Mary Barton*, Gaskell described her fiction as having been written from immersion in the 'busy streets'. But her urban *mise en scène* overwhelmingly subordinates streets and crowds to domestic spaces and family groups. Her occasional crowd scenes are designed to show that people become unreadable (if not, as in the case of the mill riot in *North and South*, de-characterised) in the streets. Hence the narrator's observation in *Mary Barton* that 'he could not, you cannot, read the lot of those who daily pass you by in the street. How do you know the wild romances of their lives; the trials, the temptations they are even now enduring, resisting, sinking under?', which tellingly begins 'He wondered if any in all the hurrying crowd had come from such a house' as his (*MB*, 101).

While Levine uses this passage to argue that Gaskell insists that we cannot know the many, I suggest that she is arguing that it was impossible to know the many *in the streets*.[42]

In Gaskell's fiction, visiting proliferates not least because it provides opportunities to develop social knowledge not otherwise available. Instances range from the formal sick-nurse visits of Ruth Hilton, through the almost conventional ladies' visiting of Margaret Hale and then of Thornton to the Higginses, to a range of variants: the Bartons' visiting of the Davenports, Ellinor Wilkins' philanthropic visits in *A Dark Night's Work*, Tom Fletcher's help in the house across his court in 'Hand and Heart'. Visiting brings visibility. Manchester begins to become legible for Margaret Hale when the 'desolate crowded streets' (*MB*, 288) are replaced by the Higgins' cottage.[43] In the case of Thornton's visits to Higgins, the narrator's commentary could hardly be more emphatic: through his visiting Thornton is 'brought face to face, man to man, with an individual of the masses around him, and (take notice) *out* of the character of master and workman'; thus, they can begin to recognise each other as human beings (*N&S*, 511, emphasis in original). He also gets to know of the existence of Margaret's brother Frederick, and hence the removal of his suspicion of her conduct. Even Ruth's visiting, which offers little sense of her personal learning, operates (along with her work in the fever ward to which it leads) as a mechanism of revelation, presenting and vindicating her character.

Gaskell's composition aligns tightly with the key components of the visiting mode: observation, tableau and specimen. Her picture of Manchester was, as she stressed, based on 'personal observation', and the praise of Gaskell's 'observant eye' was an almost universal response of her reviewers.[44] Gaskell was unwilling to trespass on matters 'the details of which I never saw'.[45] Her characters insistently privilege sight as a mode of knowing. 'I'm wanting in learning, I'm aware', confesses Job Legh, 'but I can use my eyes' (*MB*, 456). 'I believe what I see and no more', as Bessy Higgins puts it (*N&S*, 133); similarly, Higgins tells Mr Hale that it is hard to base beliefs 'on sayings and maxims and promises made by folk yo' never saw, about the things and life yo' never saw... where's the proof?' (*N&S*, 289). Not only this, but Gaskell frequently recurred to the conventional visitors' aspiration that her readers might 'really see the scenes I tried to describe'.[46] In a direct echo of George Buckland's comment (above [p. 21]), one of her reviewers praised Gaskell's ability to persuade her readers to forget technicalities 'and to follow her through the dwellings of the rich and poor, till they are impressed by what they see and hear'.[47]

The result was the presentation of a series of set-piece tableaux, meticulously detailed interiors which contrast starkly with her underdelineated public space, with its generic long rows of housing and its featureless 'busy-ness'. Most recognisably perhaps in the opening picture of the Bartons' house in chapter 2 of *Mary Barton*, 'a complete and most admirable piece of Dutch painting', commented one review, 'which for the accuracy of its details respecting the habits and economy of the poor might almost be studied by the collector of social statistics'.[48] Froude remarked that reading *North and South* 'gave me such a strange feeling to see our drawing room *photographed* as the Hales'.[49] At points, the novels almost begin to feel like a sequence of such vignettes, the Bartons' initial house, the Davenport's cellar, the Carsons' drawing room, the second Barton house and the Wilsons' home.[50]

These set pieces function as Wardian cases for the display of Gaskell's specimens, for the creation of exactly that sort of 'natural history of our social classes' that George Eliot called for in 1856. The need for the individual to speak for a wider generality was, of course, intrinsic to social realism; but this was a particular motif of Gaskell's work, developed in conscious hostility to alternative modes of statistical abstraction. As was later said, Gaskell 'knew' the working classes 'as an ardent naturalist knows the flora of his [sic] own neighbourhood'.[51] John Barton is emblematic here; though his status is replicated by Higgins in *North and South*, through whom Thornton 'starting from a kind of friendship with the one, [became] acquainted with the many' (*N&S*, 524). Barton is introduced as 'a thorough specimen of a Manchester man' (*MB*, 41), his character and modes of speech 'exactly a poor man I know'.[52] Far from being declassed, as Steinlight has recently suggested, or merely offering what Levine terms 'a glimpse of unending particularity', Barton is 'representative', albeit not of a homogeneous, aggregated class, and is recognisable to contemporaries as such; 'his class, his order, was what he stood by, not the rights of his own paltry self' (*MB*, 220).[53]

If we have any doubts about Gaskell's taxonomic procedure here, they should be dispelled by the figure of Job Legh in *Mary Barton*, one of those working-class entomologists who 'pore over every new specimen with real scientific delight' (*MB*, 75); and another character drawn from a specific working-class model.[54] The symbolic and structural load Legh carries in *Mary Barton* has been widely recognised.[55] He serves as a representative of a 'class of men in Manchester unknown even to many the inhabitants', of the limits of existing social knowledge; as an alternative working-class 'type' (in the distinctive sense articulated by Lukács),[56] of the autodidact Manchester mechanic, with his fascination for learning of all sorts, his 'love of hard words' (314), his smatterings of knowledge, which challenges the collapsing of workers identities into occupation.[57] And he acts as a representative of a regime of knowledge whose classificatory protocols, increasingly a matter of debate even in the years before Darwin's *Origin of Species*, relied heavily on the accumulations of specimens which could manifest both type, and degrees of variation around that type. In this context, the argument Legh has with the sailor Will Wilson, over the existence of mermaids, can be seen as a deliberate exploration of the tensions of hearsay, observation and specimen. Observation can degenerate into hearsay when retold, but the specimen provides portable and replicable proof (*MB*, 199–203).[58]

Reading homes

The extract from Ebenezer Elliott, the 'Corn Law Rhymer', which serves as an epigram to chapter 5 of *Mary Barton* in which Job Legh is introduced, is significant for its explicit equation of the naturalist's recognition and delineation of species with knowledge of each animal's 'home and history' (just as George Eliot's idealised natural history was presented as beginning with 'the degree to which [the social classes] are influenced by local conditions').[59] In the same way that nineteenth-century natural history was increasingly a spatialised science whose professionalisation was associated with rigorous attention to the locations at which specimens were found and collected, so Gaskell's practice as a 'visiting mode' novelist culminates in the primacy afforded to the reading of homes and then their mapping.[60]

Housing looms large in both novels and short stories, many, perhaps most, of which begin or end with a house move, or a description of houses as a way of fixing the scene. The degree of prominence given is hard to exaggerate. Jem's proposal to Mary offers his home before his heart (*MB*, 174), just as Ruth's suitor Jerry Dixon offers her 'a four-roomed house, and furniture comfortable; and eighty pounds a year' (*Ruth*, 117). Houses embody social status. The Manchester working classes registered the increasing wealth of their employers in their 'removing from house to house, each one grander than the last, till he ends in building one more magnificent than all, … or sells his mill to buy an estate in the country' (*MB*, 59), just as in 'A Manchester Marriage' prosperity and poverty is inscribed in successive house moves. The description of the Davenports' cellar in *Mary Barton* is a set piece of Gaskell's social reportage, but its significance is its contribution to a differentiated working class, part of the social gradation from the Bartons, to the Wilsons, to the Davenports.

This approach invests homes with extraordinary power and resonance. Esther, as a fallen woman, cannot bring herself to cross the threshold (*MB*, 213), just as John Barton clings to his home because of its reminders of his wife. In this sense, *pace* Steinlight, individuals become outsiders or supernumeraries not when they are jobless, but when they are homeless. Esther's social position in the first few pages of *Mary Barton* is characterised as 'street walker', and is further placed by her absence from the domestic party at the Bartons' house. As she tells Jem, 'Decent good people have homes. We have none' (*MB*, 214). Without a home, she is 'wandering' and unlocatable, and can 'never more belong' to the working 'class' (*MB*, 171, 292).[61] More than this, homes provide more reliable evidence than personal appearance of an individual's history and character, 'thick', as Josie Billington has put it, 'with the cumulative deposits of the past'.[62] Homes give specificity, separate the individual from the mass; they stand metonymically for households and so for people. Part of Mr Hale's 'Southernness' was his incapacity to read the houses of the working classes of Milton (see his visit to Boucher, *N&S*, 212), and perhaps Gaskell shared some sense of the alienness of working-class houses; however, despite any initial impression of homogeneity given (the 'long rows of small houses, with a blank wall here and there' which describes Marlborough Street where Thornton lives in *N&S*, 157), she repeatedly enforced the indexical character of houses and homes. Attention, in what Uglow describes as the 'almost anthropological accounts' of homes, is lavished on the 'evidences of character in inanimate things' (*Ruth*, 165):[63] the Hale drawing room, the Holman home in *Cousin Phillis*, the seamstresses' room at the start of *Ruth*.

The home of a stranger encountered in 'Lizzie Leigh', 'exquisitely clean and neat in outward appearance: threshold, window, and window-sill', offered 'outward signs of some spirit of purity within' (*FSS*, 55). Gaskell is acutely aware of the exhibitionary function of furniture and furnishings, both as extension of personality and as status signifier. The Bartons' status as respectable and conscientious workers was embodied in their house and its 'many conveniences', the fire in the grate ready to be fanned into vigour, candles to aid the firelight, check curtains, geraniums, rooms 'crammed with furniture' (*MB*, 49–50), as was Alice Wilson's in 'the perfect cleanliness' of her cellar, though much more sparsely furnished and damp (65–6). Hence the significance of the pawning away of the Davenport's possessions, the Wilsons' withered window plants or the gradual deterioration of the Bartons' house, as 'by degrees [it] was stripped of its little ornaments' (158–9).[64] Neglect registered in dirt and cold. Characters are defined far more by their attention to domestic duties than by formal occupational or economic *circumstances*. This is a particular theme of *Ruth*, manifest in the inscribed labour of the Benson kitchen 'with the well-scoured dresser, the shining saucepans, the well-blacked grate, and whitened hearth, which seemed to rise up from the very flags and ruddily cheer the most distant corners' (265).[65] Such is the strength of the expectation of homology, that when it breaks down, and individuals offer misleading indications of their residences, it is noteworthy (*N&S*, 157).

This puts Gaskell at odds with any rigid sense of the geographical situatedness of status: Barton (though she accepts a certain atypicality in this) allows poverty to register in decay not relocation. But it also reinforces the sense to which social identity comes as much from residence as from occupation or income.[66] Hence Gaskell's description of John Barton as 'born of factory workers, and himself bred up in youth, and living in manhood, among the mills', so that he is, as Steinlight notes, representative of his class genealogically and environmentally.[67] Hence also the way Barton conceives of his fellow chartists not as fellow workers but as 'neighbours' (130, viz 241), a collectivity which is registered, for example, in the neighbour, a stranger to the house, new to the district, and yet still pitching in to look after Mrs Boucher in the aftermath of the news of the death of her husband (*N&S*, 371).

Gaskell's cartographic imaginary

The spatial dynamics of Gaskell's fiction are usually conceived of on a broader scale (north versus south, country versus city), than on these sorts of 'micro-spatialities', and recent attention has been given more to networks and circulations, to movement between rather than places within.[68] Edgar Wright went so far as to suggest, not entirely unfairly, that what Gaskell offered 'is not Manchester the city but Manchester the symbol of a type of background for living'.[69] Yet, Gaskell was acutely aware of the need for 'some definite, coloured, living idea' of cities, of the importance of the experienced landscape, 'to understand how such a little clause as "It is but a stone's throw" helps us to hear and read and think'. During her visit to Rome in 1856, she spent a great deal of time studying maps of the city, while recognising that this still did not enable her to grasp much of its actual lived experience, including 'relative positions (such as what can be seen from the other?)'.[70] In Manchester, as in Rome, this gap required the development of an imagined cartography.

Gaskell grounds her Manchester fiction in significant local allusion. Admittedly, this is largely a reality effect, which anchors the setting in respect of the conventional geographies of Victorian urban description.[71] This is true of the incidental locations of *Mary Barton*, the 'respectable little street leading off Ardwick Green' where Mary is apprenticed as dressmaker (63); Oxford Street where George Wilson drops down dead (*MB*, 141); 'Turner Street', where Carson is murdered (which was a street in the Shudehill area, not in reality 'a lonely unfrequented way' (*MB*, 261), but a minor thoroughfare with beerhouses, fronting on one the cholera nests of the 1849 outbreak). Yet, this sort of placing imitates the strategies of other forms of visiting reportage and trades on this notoriety. And so, for example, the address of the Davenport cellar in Berry Street, off Store Street, places it at a spot featured repeatedly in contemporary accounts of Manchester 'slums'.[72]

But true to her desire to present sociological complexity, Gaskell's urban society is not primarily characterised by the sort of social segregation often presented as the structuring reality in early statistical accounts. Thornton lives in the precincts of his mill. Carson lives in one of the suburban villas beyond the working-class houses, 'almost in the country' (*MB*, 105, viz *N&S*, 267), but it is accessible to Barton, part of a sequence which includes the serried rows of working-class streets, the gradations of front and back streets, the outer courts opening off 'a squalid street' (*N&S*, 132) and the inner courts off which is the Barton house. The overall effect generates the concentrated and complicated juxtapositions which place the shops of London Road five minutes from the abject squalor of Berry Street.

For all this, there is little sense of the social topography of the city. We are offered colour but not a developed spatial structure; little beyond the broad distinctions of commercial centre and working-class residential districts, between Deansgate and Ancoats. There is a suggestion of districts associated with degraded character, as in the house at which Bellingham met Ruth, 'in the lowest part of the town, where all the bad characters haunt', as it was described (75), or a presentation of the concentration of fever in a 'miserable living, filthy neighbourhood' (99). Esther's temporary address in Nicholas Street, Angel's [sic] Meadow, tallies with the district's reputation as the main location of Manchester's common lodging houses; although this is not spelled out. We never know precisely where the Wilsons' or the Bartons' live, nor do we get an explicit mapping of the progression of poverty from Barton to Wilson to Davenport.

Perhaps it is simply that Gaskell chooses to sacrifice imaginative mapping to facilitate an emphasis on the unknowability of the city, its amorphous and occlusive qualities, what Catherine Gallagher has described as 'the constantly obstructed passage through Manchester's chaotic squalor'.[73] In this way, the 'well-known' Greenheys Fields which open *Mary Barton* soon give way to the Bartons' home, whose location is difficult to know: those following to the house 'through many half-finished streets, all alike one another', dark and misty even as the fields were bathed in early evening sunshine, 'might easily have been bewildered and lost [their] way' (*MB*, 48, viz 171). Rushing to Carson's mill, built in the old part of town where the first mills were built, amid 'the crowded alleys and back streets of the neighbourhood', to see the fire there, Mary and her friend Margaret are 'Guided by the ruddy light more than by any exact knowledge of the streets that led to the mill' (*MB*, 87). Even the nearest doctor to whom John Barton runs in haste when his wife's labour goes wrong, needs to be guided to his house. Gaskell does not ignore the elements of neighbourhood solidarity that provide networks of information and also a degree of insulation from outside incursion. And she gives a sense of shape and structure to the city which contrasts strongly with the sense of overwhelming strangeness which is often the dominant note of the accounts of visitors to the city. But her instincts, not just in her prostitution plotlines, are towards anonymity, and the capacity of the city to swallow and lose. Nicholas Higgins is not to be found while his daughter lies dying.

Conclusion

Gaskell was a novelist of the visiting mode. She argued for visiting not only as a treatment for contemporary ignorance, but also as a fundamental nexus in the generation of social action. As Dorice Williams Elliott observes, her urban fiction represents the novel 'as a philanthropic act akin to visiting'. She encouraged readerly responses of both knowing and doing, 'exciting the mind to a better knowledge and a more active remedial interference on behalf of the labouring classes'.[74] In doing so, she offered, as Caroline Levine has recently observed, 'a critique of the mastery implied by statistical knowledge'; not as the product of an 'enormity effect', nor by adopting biopower's organising tropes, as Steinlight has argued,[75] but by challenging the methods of early Victorian social science and its claims to describe society through abstracted populations.[76] The fundamental nature of this challenge is registered in the hostility to her fiction manifest in the contemporary responses of liberal economists and statisticians, and the defences mounted by visiting institutions and their representatives.

Contemporary reviews of Gaskell's works rehearsed the conflicts over the forms of social knowledge in which she had intervened. While sympathetic reviewers praised the intimacy of her information, and the clarity of her illustration, more statistically inclined reviewers like the ex-cotton master and one of the founders of the Manchester Statistical Society, W.R. Greg, launched a wholesale challenge both to Gaskell's taxonomies and her underlying epistemologies. Particular fire was directed at her specimens. Greg rejected John Barton as 'a fair representative of the artisans and factory operatives of Manchester', and presented Gaskell as exposed 'to the charge of culpable misrepresentation'; and similar criticisms were directed at *North and South*, whose problem, thought the radical *Leader*, was that the Higginses and Thorntons 'are not types, nor even generalities'.[77] Gaskell's temerity in intervening beyond the new circles of professional expertise drew similar fire. For the representatives of social science 'if there are two classes that should give trade and masters-and-men questions a wide birth those classes are clergymen and women'. 'Some of those representations of factory life which have passed current as authentic representations of fact', argued a review in the *British Quarterly Review* (edited by Robert Vaughan, another Manchester School radical), 'have been based on representations and fabrications obtained in the most disreputable manner through paid agents, sent to collect all they could that would tend to blacken the character of various leading men connected with manufactures'.[78] When the *Manchester Guardian* challenged both the accuracy and the representativeness of Gaskell's account, tellingly counterpointing her evidence with a factory-based survey, we should not be surprised that the first to spring to her defence was David Winstanley, secretary of the Miles Platting Mechanics' Institute, closely aligned to the Ministry to the Poor, and himself an active visitor to the Manchester poor.[79]

Notes

1 Beth Fowkes Tobin, *Superintending the Poor. Charitable Ladies and Paternal Landlords in British Fiction, 1770–1860* (1993), 129; Siegel, *Charity and Condescension*, 170, n6.

2 See the discussions in Tobin, *Superintending the Poor*, 143–4, Goodlad, *Victorian State*, 109–11.

3 G. Jewsbury, *Marian Withers* (1851), I, 15; letter of 19 October 1849, in Mrs Alexander Ireland, ed., *Selections from the Letters of Geraldine Endsor Jewsbury to Jane Welsh Carlyle* (1892), 306.

4 Gaskell was not particular about distinguishing towns and cities, in *Cranford* 'Drumble', another of her names for Manchester, is also 'the great neighbouring commercial town', 39.

5 All three are included in *Elizabeth Gaskell. Four Short Stories*, introduced by Anna Walters (1993), to which subsequent inline references refer (*FSS*). Subsequent references to *Mary Barton* and *North and South* are to the Penguin English Library editions, edited by Stephen Gill and Martin Dodsworth, respectively. The discussion also encompasses other writings such as the indeterminate 'Hand and Heart', *Sunday School Penny Magazine*, in five parts: July–December 1849.

6 Further references are to the Penguin English Library editions, *Cranford/Cousin Phillis*, edited by Peter Keating, and *Ruth*, edited by Alan Shelston.

7 A point made by Seed, 'Antinomies of Liberal Culture', 19–20.

8 Mat Hompes, 'Mrs Gaskell', *Gentleman's Magazine* CCLXXIX (1895).

9 See letter to Dickens, in *Four Short Stories*, 11.

10 According to an allusion in H.C. Irvine, *The Old D.P.S.* ([1933]), 9, cited John Geoffrey Sharps, *Mrs. Gaskell's Observation and Invention: A Study of Her Non-Biographic Works* (1970), 57. For later passing reference to visiting (during the cotton famine), see Jenny Uglow, *Elizabeth Gaskell. A Habit of Stories* (1993), 319.

11 There are various references, including 'A Manchester Correspondent' (Mat Hompes), 'Mrs. Gaskell and Her Social Work among the Poor', *The Inquirer and Christian Life* (London), 8 October 1910, A. Cobden Smith 'Mrs Gaskell and Lower Mosley Street', *The Sunday School Quarterly* (January 1911), 156–61, which included a tribute to 'her kindly and unselfish labours among the homes of our scholars', 156. See also the notice in *Unitarian Herald*, 17 November 1865 (possibly by James Martineau), quoted in A. Easson, *Elizabeth Gaskell: The Critical Heritage, 1848–1910* (1991), 506.

12　William Gaskell was on the committee from the beginning, secretary from 1841. For his prominence and influence in the M&SSA, see Margaret Shaen, *Memorials of Two Sisters: Susanna and Catherine Winkworth* (1908), 93.

13　Gaskell to Vernon Lushington (c.9 April 1862), John Chapple and Alan Shelston, eds, *Further Letters of Mrs Gaskell* (2013), 235–6.

14　See Uglow, *Elizabeth Gaskell*, 163, quoting Susanna Winkworth to Emily Winkworth, 1846, Susanna Winkworth and Margaret Shaen, eds, *Letters and Memorials of Catherine Winkworth* (2 vols, 1883–6), I, 106–7.

15　See the reference to the visiting of Madge, along with Brooke Herford, another of the teachers, in A. Cobden Smith, 'Brooke Herford', *Sunday School Quarterly* 1 (1909), 118–19, and Brooke Herford, *Travers Madge: A Memoir* (1867); also John Chapple and Arthur Pollard, *The Letters of Mrs Gaskell* (1966), L677; and recommended as someone 'living right amongst them', *Further Letters*, 238. Uglow comments that Madge 'roused Elizabeth into far greater involvement than before', Uglow, *Elizabeth Gaskell*, 156.

16　See the letter from Susanna to Emily Winkworth, 8 June 1849, Shaen, *Memorials*, 45–6, 96–8.

17　It is significantly often given priority, as in her discussion of responses to the visiting of the Brontes, 'to inquire into their condition, to counsel, or to admonish them', *The Life of Charlotte Bronte*, Elizabeth Jay, ed. (1857), 42.

18　For links with Reach see Carolyn Lambert, *The Meanings of Home in Elizabeth Gaskell's Fiction* (2013), 109. On the Domestic Mission, see M.C. Fryckstedt, *Elizabeth Gaskell's 'Mary Barton' and 'Ruth': A Challenge to Liberal England*, *Studia Anglistica Upsaliensia* 43 (1982), 90–7. Note direct quotes from Layhe's 1842 report of certain passages. In a similar way, Gaskell's account of the 'fever' hospital in *Ruth* drew explicitly and extensively on procedures at the Manchester Royal Infirmary and Manchester House of Recovery, Katherine Inglis, 'Unimagined Community and Disease in *Ruth*', in Lesa Scholl and Emily Morris, eds, *Place and Progress in the Works of Elizabeth Gaskell* (2015), 67–82, especially 71–4.

19　See two very illuminating letters, Gaskell to Charles Bosanquet, 7 November 1859, *Letters*, L446a, and Gaskell to S.A. Steinthal, n.d. (but probably early 1860s), *ibid*, L630.

20　John Gross, 'Mrs Gaskell', in Ian Watt, ed., *The Victorian Novel. Modern Essays in Criticism* (1971).

21　Gaskell to Edward Holland, 13 January 1849, *Letters*, L39a; see Gaskell to Mrs Greg, *Letters*, L42; see also Gaskell to John Seely Hart, 28 April 1850, *Letters*, L71; Gaskell to Lady Kay-Shuttleworth, 16 July 1850, *Letters*, L72a.

22　'The great beauty of this "Tale of Manchester Life" consists in its self-evident truthfulness', *The Inquirer*, 11 November 1848. Likewise the verdict of the *Christian Reformer* (1848) that 'characters are natural, life-like, and very various', 747.

23　Charles Kingsley in *Fraser's Magazine* (April 1849), Easson, *Critical Heritage*, 153–4.

24　For recent criticism which takes up this theme, see for example, Eleanor Courtemanche, *The 'Invisible Hand' and British Fiction, 1818–1860* (2011), which replicates at a number of points the analysis advanced here; Gregory Vargo, 'Questions from Workers Who Read; Education and Self-Formation in Chartist Print Culture and Elizabeth Gaskell's *Mary Barton*', in his *An Underground History of Early Victorian Fiction. Chartism, Radical Print Culture, and the Social Problem Novel* (2018), 115–47.

25 *Examiner*, 21 April 1855, in Easson, *Critical Heritage*, 340. As Canon Richard Parkinson had put it, '*information* will cure what *ignorance* has caused', Parkinson, *Present Condition*, 15.

26 See the discussion in A. Easson, *Elizabeth Gaskell* (1979), and its reference to a letter describing Barton as 'the bewildered life of an ignorant thoughtful man of strong power of sympathy', 76.

27 See the discussion in Hilary Schor, *Scheherazade in the Marketplace. Elizabeth Gaskell and the Victorian Novel* (1992), 30–1; a position consistent with the conclusions of D. Churchill, *Crime Control and Everyday Life in the Victorian City*, (2018), 64–9, but also at odds with Gaskell's brief essay 'Disappearances', *Household Words* (7 June 1851), 246–50.

28 See the discussion in Dorice Williams Elliott, 'The Female Visitor and the Marriage of Classes in Gaskell's *North and South*', *Nineteenth Century Literature* 49 (1994), 21–49; as Courtemanche notes, in Gaskell's fiction mediations between self and collective 'are explicitly framed as a problem in political economy', Courtemanche, *The 'Invisible Hand'*, 173. Inevitably this leads to parallels with the position George Eliot develops in 'The Natural History of German Life', with its rejection of 'The tendency created by the splendid conquests of modern generalisation to believe that all social questions are merged in economical science, and that the relations of men to their neighbours may be settled by algebraic equations', *Essays and Leaves from a Notebook* (1884), 238.

29 Uglow, *Gaskell*, 374–5. For this privileging of 'practical knowledge and … experience' over 'fine names and … theories', see also *Mr Harrison's Confessions* (411).

30 This implies the sort of practical rule-of-thumb knowledge that James C. Scott has described as 'mētis', *Seeing Like a State* (1998), 311–13.

31 Caroline Levine, 'The Enormity Effect: Realist Fiction, Literary Studies and the Refusal to Count', *Genre* 50.1 (April 2017), 61–75.

32 See Siegel, *Charity and Condescension*, 51–2, and Jonathan V. Farina, '"A Certain Shadow": Personified Abstractions and the Form of *Household Words*', *Victorian Periodicals Review* 42 (2009), 392–415, which outlines the broad consistency of Dickens' instincts with Gaskell's; significantly 'Lizzie Leigh' launched the first issue of *Household Words*, which also published a number of the other short stories drawn on here.

33 As in the comments in *Ruth*, 10, and the vignette in *A Dark Night's Work*, 120. In this, while agreeing with Audrey Jaffe that it is a central dynamic of Victorian fiction to identify a norm and explore deviations from it, I reject the suggestion that discussions of normality are necessarily inflected with specifically statistical understandings, Audrey Jaffe, *The Affective Life of the Average Man. The Victorian Novel and the Stock Market Graph* (2010).

34 Patsy Stoneman points out how closely this approach aligns with Gaskell's father's exposure of what she describes as 'the apparent mathematical certainty of "political economy" as a cheat. Attacking "political economists" in their own terms, he had shown them to be "blind guides to the mazes of this science"', Stoneman, *Elizabeth Gaskell* (2006), 87.

35 This theme is also explored on several levels in Gaskell's 'The Heart of John Middleton'.

36 Echoed in Margaret's musings on Frederick's position as a Spanish merchant (*N&S*, 425). Just as there is a motif of the inner person often hidden by the face they present to the world, for example Margaret's conversation with her servant Martha, and Mr Hale and his friends (*N&S*, 427–30).

37 Emily Steinlight, *Populating the Novel. Literary Form and the Politics of Surplus Life* (2018), 110; or indeed that *'Mary Barton* shows that making remainders rather than representing a consistent class of workers, is what industrial fiction and social science share', 97.

38 'So much for generalities', as the narrator observes, after a long discussion of the dynamics of striking 'Let us now return to individuals' (*MB*, 223).

39 A point made by Alan Shelston in his *'Ruth*: Mrs Gaskell's Neglected Novel', *Bulletin of the John Rylands Library* 58.1 (1975), 173–92.

40 Uglow, *Gaskell*, 195.

41 And taken up by later accounts, including Crosfield, *Bitter Cry*, 9, 12.

42 Levine, 'Enormity Effect', 63.

43 As Uglow suggests, *Gaskell*, 372.

44 Gaskell to Mrs Greg, early 1849, *Letters*, L49. How could she, she asked Lady Kay-Shuttleworth, write about potential employers' responses 'the details of which I never saw', *Letters*, L72a; Edgeworth to Mary Holland, 27 December 1848, quoted Easson, *Critical Heritage*, 89; for one such description of her style as 'full of life and colour, betraying a quick observant eye', see *Prospective Review* XVII (February 1849), 41.

45 Gaskell to Lady Kay-Shuttleworth, 16 July (?1850), *Letters*, L72a. In the same way she praises Margaret Howitt's writing in that she 'does not make the reader see the things with your eyes, but you present the scene itself to him', Margaret Howitt, *Mary Howitt, Her Autobiography* (1889), II, 66.

46 Gaskell to Eliza Fox, 29 May 1849, *Letters*, L48; double underlined in original, see Sharps, *Observation and Invention*, 61.

47 *Eclectic Review*, 25 (January 1849), quoted Easson, *Critical Heritage*, 96; the review later talks about Gaskell 'leading us amongst them, and making us spectators of their pleasures and their cares', 97.

48 *Prospective Review*, XVII (February 1849), 42. For similar comments, see the review of *The Moorland Cottage*, *The Leader*, 21 December 1850; '[Mary Barton: A Tale of Manchester Life]', *North British Review* (August 1851), 429–41.

49 Froude to Gaskell, 5 January 1862, quoted Uglow, *Gaskell*, 229.

50 Again a common theme of contemporary remark, see Easson, *Critical Heritage*, 62, 65, 68, 'homely yet vigorous painting' (John Forster in *The Examiner*, 4 November 1848, 70), 'pencillings of a true artist', *Inquirer*, 11 November 1848, in Easson, *Critical Heritage*, 75; or 'a most graphic sketch', *Sun*, 30 November 1848, *ibid*, 79.

51 William Minto in *Fortnightly Review*, ns XXIV (September 1878), 353–69, in Easson *Critical Heritage*, 553.

52 Gaskell to Eliza Fox, 29 May 1849, *Letters*, L48. The typicality of Barton was the centre of the book's authenticity for the working-class poet Samuel Bamford, who remarked 'of John Barton, I have known hundreds, his very self in all things except his fatal crime', Ross Douglas Waller, *Letters Addressed to Mrs Gaskell by Celebrated Contemporaries* (1935).

53 Levine, 'Enormity Effect', 68. See also Amy King, 'Taxonomical Cures: The Politics of Natural History and Herbalist Medicine in Elizabeth Gaskell's Mary Barton', in Noah Heringman, eds, *Romantic Science: The Literary Forms of Natural History* (2003), 262.

54 See Anne Secord, 'Elizabeth Gaskell and the Artisan Naturalists of Manchester', *Gaskell Society Journal* 19 (2005), 34–51. For a strikingly congruent argument

about the character of Roger Hamley in Gaskell's *Wives and Daughters*, see Karen Boiko, 'Reading and (Re)Writing Class: Elizabeth Gaskell's *Wives and Daughters*', *Victorian Literature and Culture* 33.1 (2005), 85–106.

55 See Danielle Coriale, 'Gaskell's Naturalist', *Nineteenth-Century Literature* 63.3 (2008), 346–75. I do not attempt to follow Coriale here in seeing natural history as representing a liberation from class constraints, or her suggestion that Legh is in tension with what she sees as Gaskell's anti-classificatory instincts.

56 As in the discussion in György Lukács, *Studies in European Realism* (2002) of the distinction between the 'type' and the 'average'. Averages flatten and homogenise. Type can be exceptional as long as it offers 'clearly revealed social determinants', 170.

57 Easson, *Critical Heritage*, 65; see the similar commentary in 'Libbie Marsh' that 'many of the weavers of Manchester know and care more about birds than anyone would easily credit' (*FSS*, 9).

58 Perhaps this is the significance of Gaskell's (otherwise) strange description of Job's antipathy to writing: 'Writing was to him little more than an auxiliary to natural history: a way of ticketing specimens, not of expressing thoughts' (*MB*, 406), a sense of the dangers that even the protocols of natural history can be reduced to the brutality of the experience of 'some insect, which [Job] was impaling on a corking-pin' (*MB*, 423).

59 Ebenezer Elliott, *The Splendid Village, Corn Law Rhymes and Other Poems*, I (1834), 25; Eliot, 'Natural History', 239.

60 See, for example, the discussion in Jim Endersby, *Imperial Science. Joseph Hooker and the Practices of Victorian Science* (2008), especially chapter 8 'Charting', 225–48.

61 The scarcity of true homelessness in Gaskell's work is discussed in Lambert, *The Meanings of Home in Elizabeth Gaskell's Fiction*, e.g. 113.

62 Josie Billington, 'Gaskell's "Rooted" Prose Realism', in Scholl and Morris, *Place and Progress*, 159–71.

63 Uglow, *Gaskell*, 122.

64 'No observant individual who has been in the habit of regularly visiting the habitations of the poor, can have failed to remark many sure indications of increasing poverty. He [sic] must often have noticed comfortably furnished houses rendered desolate by the disappearance of one article of furniture after another', Adshead, *Distress*, 47.

65 We see the same focus on cleanliness and kitchen utensils in *The Grey Woman*.

66 This is, in part, what elides the worker/non-worker distinction which exercises Steinlight, although, of course, part of the contemporary discourse was the sense of districts, of which in Manchester Angel Meadow/Charter Street became the most regularly invoked, which were (paradoxically) synonymous with homelessness (via lodging houses).

67 The 'population to which Barton belongs is thus defined by the confluence of economic relations, geography, cultural habits and biological characteristics', Steinlight, *Populating the Novel*, 99.

68 This is the overriding preoccupation of the essays in Scholl and Morris, *Place and Progress*.

69 Edgar Wright, *Mrs Gaskell. The Basis for Reassessment* (1965), 94.

70 Gaskell to Lord Stanhope, 22 January 1856, in Chapple and Shelston, *Further Letters*, 106–7.

71 A strategy discussed in T. Gilfoyle, *The City of Eros* (1992), quoted in Robert Dowling, *Slumming in New York* (2007), 4.

72 See report in M&SSA Papers, M126/2/4/1-7 (London Road), Manchester Archives.

73 C. Gallagher, *The Body Economic* (2005), 62.

74 *Eclectic Review* 25 (January 1849), quoted Easson, *Critical Heritage*, 97.

75 Levine, 'Enormity Effect', 70.

76 In this she was not alone; see, for example, the discussions in Gage McWeeny, 'The Sociology of the Novel: George Eliot's Strangers', *Novel* 42.3 (2009), 538–45, and Klotz, 'Manufacturing Fictional Individuals'.

77 W.R. Greg, *Edinburgh Review* (April 1849), and in his *Essays on Political and Social Science* (1853), I, 344–88, evinces a statistical critique, in that fundamental failure is to 'give exceptional cases as a fair type of the generality', *ibid*, 117; *The Leader*, 14 April 1855, printed Easson, *Critical Heritage*, 333–7, quote at 333. Compare with the passing comment of Thomas Ballantyne, Anti-Corn Law Leaguer and one of the original owners of the *Manchester Examiner*, who also stressed the difference of Higgins in a system 'the fatal tendency' of which is 'to destroy the individuality of the workman and render him a powerless unit in a gregarious crowd', *Blackwood's Edinburgh Magazine* January 1856, extracted in Easson, *Critical Heritage*, 368.

78 *British Quarterly Review*, in Easson, *Critical Heritage*, 103–4.

79 Editorial, *MG*, 28 February 1849, and Winstanley's response, *MG*, 7 March 1849 (which prompted a further editorial response enforcing that what is at issue is the generality of Gaskell's critique). For Winstanley see E. and T. Kelly, eds, *A Schoolmaster's Notebook* (1957).

5 The case of educational reform

Prevalence and persistence

All of the components of the visiting mode are visible in the campaigns for educational reform in Victorian Britain. Education emerged in the 1830s and 1840s as one of the raft of reforming measures required to address the social dysfunctionality of the Victorian city. Inevitably, it was a key focus of the early activities of the MSS: a number of the society's most prominent early investigations focused on educational deficiencies, including its reports on education in Manchester (1834), Salford (1835), Bury (1835), Liverpool (1836) and York (1837). In some respects, the MSS did temporarily create an approach which transcended denominational difference and sustained an aggregated rhetoric of insufficiency. The society's inquiries led to the formation in 1837 with great fanfare of the Manchester Society for Promoting National Education which opened two schools in working-class districts of Manchester, although it was only possible to sustain the schools for six and four years, respectively.

But if this approach was briefly dominant, it was steadily undermined from the late 1830s as the politics of educational reform hardened along denominational lines. As the debate over educational provision reignited in the mid-1840s, questions of geographic distribution gained prominence.[1] Associations supporting the extension of education in the 1840s were inexorably drawn to recognition of the paucity (if not absence) of educational institutions in many of the poorer working-class districts.[2] In the 1840s, all sides cited as the fundamental problem that there were whole districts in Manchester destitute of education.[3] Debate was fuelled by the failure to establish spatially stable categories of judgement. Absolute standards were elusive; instead, considerable allowance was made for variations in the nature of the district in which the schools were situated, and hence in the character of the population from which the children were drawn.[4] Although the rival schemes which emerged from Manchester, the secular Lancashire (later National) Public Schools Association and the denominational Manchester and Salford Education Bill Committee scheme disputed the extent to which it could be argued that the various districts of Manchester were already sufficiently provided with school accommodation, both groups recognised the geographical dimension of the problem.[5] From the outset, the National Public Schools Association (NPSA) was driven by the conviction that, as one supporter put it, 'the efforts of sects and parties always left large and necessitous districts neglected'.[6] While Anglican campaigners sought to focus on the need for greater government support for existing schools, their argument was essentially parallel: that government assistance was needed in the poorer districts where the limited ability of parents to pay, and of schools to raise voluntary contributions, made it harder to sustain educational provision.[7] Although the quality of schooling was never entirely marginalised in this debate, the exchanges recorded by the Select Committee on Education in Manchester and Salford in 1852 and 1853 turned incessantly on debates over what should count as effective participation in education, along with attempts to map educational provision and define the areas in which it was insufficient.[8]

The educational controversy helped to undermine the ability of the Manchester Statistical Society to act as neutral ground. But the decline of the Statistical Society did not indicate any lessening of the statistical imperative. The educational debate was essentially (or essentially resolved into) a statistical debate. It was entirely characteristic that the initial circular of the Manchester Education Aid Society (EAS) when it formed in the 1860s was headed 'Statistics of Education in Manchester and Salford'.[9] It is important not to underestimate the extent of the investigative activity that the debates over education prompted from the later 1840s into the 1870s. In the later 1840s, the promoters of Pendleton Mechanics' Institute made a house-to-house inquiry about literacy levels in the district to ascertain the extent of educational need.[10] Very soon after its establishment, the Lancashire Public Schools Association organised investigations of conditions in Ancoats and then in other districts in Manchester, later followed by detailed surveys of the St John's and St Michael's wards, and these inquiries were followed by similar studies by the Manchester and Salford Education Bill Committee and the rival, more-informally organised supporters of the denominational voluntary schools, the results of which formed the basis of much of the evidence presented to the 1852–3 Select Committee on Education in Manchester and Salford.[11] These investigations were renewed intermittently through the 1850s and early 1860s.[12] In the early 1850s, the Church party undertook a number of linked inquiries, including visits to 17,426 families in selected districts of the city.[13] City missionaries provided the proportions of children not receiving education, as well as information about provision at a local level.[14] During the 1850s, the existence of large tracts of the city marked out by lack of educational provision became the central plank of the NPSA campaign.[15]

A significant aspect of these debates was the limited purchase that the apparatus of state inspection of education had on the public debate. The extensive published reports of the inspectors primarily focused on brief assessments of individual schools; apart from the partial exception of the Royal Commissions, there was no attempt to collect comprehensive statistical information and only the most cautious attempts at summative commentary. When W.J. Kennedy, inspector of Church of England schools for Lancashire, eventually intervened in the debates over educational insufficiency in the 1860s, his contribution was both belated and half-hearted.[16] Annual newspaper coverage of the inspectors' reports made little impression on the wider public.[17] Instead, house-to-house visitation remained conceptually and methodologically dominant, underpinned, in education as in sanitation, by the investigative machinery of the visiting associations. Not only did the NPSA witnesses to the select committee cite the evidence of city missionaries and of John Layhe, they even went as far as to suggest that the missionaries might be most effectively used as attendance officers under any rate-supported system of education.[18] Investigations by the voluntarists into the educational provision of Manchester in the 1850s included a 1,000 family survey across 20 districts conducted by MCM missionaries.[19] The Ministry to the Poor co-operated with a number of such inquiries, several of which derived from the activities of associations or campaigns that themselves owed much to the activity of the visiting associations, most importantly those of the Education Aid Society. On this basis, it is difficult to accept arguments that the limits of survey work were based on the lack of institutional capacity; it was not that there was no institutional basis, but that the nature of the basis encouraged particular ways of doing and seeing.

The brief but significant career of the Manchester and Salford Education Aid Society which drew together the NPSA party and many of the supporters of the Manchester and Salford Education Bill Committee brings many of these themes into sharp focus. The EAS was a classic of Victorian philanthropic hybridity, an attempt at direct action to enhance educational provision, a large-scale social experiment into the limits of voluntary effort and simultaneously a mechanism of social investigation. Drawing inspiration from a pilot association established in the 1850s, itself operated in close co-operation with the MCM,[20] the EAS sought to raise and distribute funds to families whose poverty prevented them from meeting the full cost of educating their children. Significantly, unlike the pressure groups of a decade previously, the EAS, although not without its critics, was able to build a broad political and religious consensus in support of its activities and findings. Its supporters included not only stalwarts of the NPSA campaigns such as the Nonconformist minister William McKerrow and John Watts, but also many of their former Anglican and Conservative opponents, like Canon Charles Richson and the staunchly Anglican silk manufacturer, E.R. Le Mare. An agent was employed to visit applicants for aid and assess their circumstances. The society paid school fees in full for children where household income was less than 1/9 per head, and contributed part fees above this amount. By the end of 1865, it had issued 6,000 orders, and new orders were being signed at a rate of 2–300 per week.

The EAS was inspired by Edward Brotherton, a Swedenborgian who after retiring from his silk manufacturing business in 1860 turned his attention to the promotion of education in Manchester and Salford. In a series of newspaper letters subsequently reprinted in pamphlet form,[21] Brotherton offered himself as a complex amalgam of flâneur, inspector, reformer and journalistic observer. Drawing attention to the educational deficiency he found in Manchester, Brotherton offered a fundamentally spatial analysis:

> But lest I should exhaust your patience, now that I have spoken of the district most favoured as regards schools, I will pass on to one of the neglected quarters. Going through the centre of the town to the northeast, there are the Cathedral School in Todd-street, and St. Michael's in Miller-street. On my first journey of exploration in this direction I could not believe what I can now say with greater certainty, that if you take a plan of Manchester, and trace a line from Miller-street by Red Bank (St. Thomas's School), and then to St. Catherine's, then to Osborne-street, near Collyhurst, and come into Oldham Road, touching, in returning, upon Bennett-street and Marshall-street, to Swanstreet, and so again to Miller-street, you will have represented an immense irregular square or circle, in which I could not find a single school. I cannot ascertain the exact population, but I suppose it will be from 40,000 to 50,000.[22]

Three aspects of this passage are especially symptomatic: the rhetorical inscribing of absence and ignorance on a 'plan of Manchester'; the sense of disbelief that Brotherton conjures in order to place himself at the outset with his readers in order to challenge their own assumptions; and the deployment of the languages of the 'journey of exploration'.[23] As well as the imperial inflections of such usages, of the construction of working-class districts as 'terra incognita', we need to attend fully to the implications of the formulation as registering a double geography of ignorance. Even though the overriding position of the society was that it was inability to pay as much as insufficiency of supply that was the key problem (so that greater endeavour by voluntary effort would not of itself be enough), the groups identified as having insufficient income to pay were themselves located spatially.[24]

As the EAS developed, more of its efforts were diverted into investigation. For J.A. Bremner, one of the honorary secretaries, central to the EAS's work was the way in which it 'placed very valuable statistics in the public domain'.[25] Characteristically, the society looked to house-to-house visitation, and only very belatedly turned to alternative channels of inquiry. For Brotherton, indeed, education was itself in part a conduit to greater contact between classes, schooling a *point d'appui* for visiting.[26] From the outset, the society's main agent had been tasked with furnishing effective vignettes for propaganda purposes; and Brotherton's newspaper letters used these to good effect.[27] He was also soon systematically collecting information about the families he visited with a view to its aggregation into data about educational conditions in the city. Once its initial judgements were challenged, the society launched a comprehensive canvass of Manchester and Salford. By the end of 1865, an assistant was being employed to investigate applications for aid, so that the society's main visitor could concentrate exclusively on accumulating evidence on poverty, school attendance and educational attainments.[28] Although in March 1866 attention turned briefly to an attempted comprehensive survey of existing schools, the society's efforts quickly reverted to a repetition by John Watts of his 1852–3 investigation into St Michael's and New Cross ward, which reported to the Manchester education conference in January 1868 that 45% of the population of children between 3 and 14 were neither at school nor at work.[29]

During this period there was no meaningful divide between the EAS investigations and the partially rejuvenated Manchester Statistical Society. Brotherton himself had few links with the Statistical Society coterie, and claimed not to have read the educational investigations of the 1830s until well into his campaign, and neither he nor Bremner were members before 1866.[30] But Richson had played a central role in the revitalisation of the MSS in the early 1850s, and John Watts was a prominent member and soon-to-be president. Indeed, the EAS's initial investigations prompted the Statistical Society to undertake its own three local surveys into education and other conditions in parts of Manchester and Salford during the 1860s, which firmly supported the EAS stance.[31]

Public controversy around EAS campaigns frequently involved the sorts of 'statistical skirmishes' Crook has explored in respect of public health.[32] The society's chief public opponent, Rev. Joseph Nunn, rector of St Thomas, Ardwick, waged an exhaustive war of attrition on the society's statistics from the outset (eventually in 1885 becoming chair of the Manchester School Board).[33]

The controversy involved a tortuous sequence of twists and turns, depending on what Nunn felt was the weakest point of the EAS position at any particular moment. So, while in January 1864, he challenged the EAS to substantiate its position by a house-to-house investigation,[34] by January 1866 in the face of energetic pressure on him to agree to an educational canvass of his parish, he was questioning the whole basis of such canvasses, arguing that

> 'The better sort of working people are tenacious of their family concerns. They dislike even to having a clergyman asking too many questions and taking notes, and it would be a very difficult matter for any external body to obtain the necessary minute particulars of such a canvass'.[35]

While accepting that in many respects his conflict with the EAS was not about the statistics per se, but about the inferences drawn from them – for example as to whether all children aged 3–12 not in school ought to be in school and can be described as 'neglected' or 'without education' if they are not in school – Nunn did occasionally also take more substantive issue with the information the society acquired. In one intervention in 1867, he noted that 'to produce definite statistical results from the society's statistics, what we require is a set of tables showing not only the average time which scholars spend in school, but also the proportion of scholars who get nine, eight, seven and so on, years of schooling'.[36]

Partisan statistics carried many dangers. Without doubt, by the standards of objective social science, the protocols adopted by investigators frequently left much to be desired. In the case of the EAS canvass, for example, it is unclear how the survey dealt with partial responses. Although the society's public pronouncements suggested comprehensiveness, a surviving sample slip suggests that the canvass of one district brought access to only 213 families in the 358 houses.[37] From the 1840s to the 1870s, much newsprint was devoted to the relative importance of average attendance as against numbers on the books, or the significance of mean years of school attendance as against the deviation around the mean, and the positions adopted by the rival parties correlated all too predictably with those which best served their *a priori* stance. Nevertheless, these controversies generated a reasonably self-critical, if common-sense, statistical discourse. Richson's contribution to the 1853 MSS *Transactions* raised a number of fundamental questions concerning educational statistics, including the difficulties of creating stable categories for phenomena such as 'attendance' or 'schooling', as well as, inevitably, the dangers of abstraction from geographical distributions.[38]

Geographical concerns dominated, conceptually and methodologically. Attempts at 'representative' sampling by the voluntarists in their 1,000 family survey, although there was no evidence of any attempt at randomisation, drew on districts which, it was claimed, were 'fairly spread over the borough, and take in a fair proportion of the lowest class of districts in the town'.[39] And they were not aggregated, but presented and fully identified district by district. Challenged that its evidence was drawn only from the worst districts of the city, the EAS developed an explicitly spatial sampling technique: a map of Manchester and Salford was divided into 144 equal squares, and 'when one of these squares ha[d] been visited, the next three squares on every side [were] passed over, until a second course of visitation [brought] the visitor into one of the intermediate squares'.[40] The process, it was noted, could be progressively extended until the whole of the city had been investigated. (This did not stop Nunn challenging the reliability of the EAS statistics precisely because the process appeared to abstract the individual cases from their specific locations within the city. It was not clear, he argued, 'where these working people were found, and how far they were representatives of the working population'; 'no particular district furnished the report, but an aggregate of cases in different localities', and on this basis, 'The whole of the Society's statistics of this kind must be set aside. It is impossible to test their accuracy or estimate their value'.[41]) There was even, belatedly, some attempt to address the limits of surveys of the whole school-age population by assessing the acquired educational standards of post-school-age children, though the relative paucity of such attempts, and their reliance on investigation of the attainments of siblings of children identified by the society agent, testify strongly to the hold the visitation mode had on investigative practices at this point.[42]

In an almost pre-programmed failure to provide a voluntaristic solution to the educational crisis, the EAS found it impossible to sustain the contributions required to meet the ever-expanding calls on its support. Its position can hardly have been helped by the diversion of its energies into campaigning, and its increasing identification as a *parti pris* association. A crisis was reached in 1867, when the canvass for new cases was halted, the staff of visitors was cut back and then the granting of new support orders was entirely suspended. Funding for existing children was largely maintained, albeit at a dwindling rate, until final closure in 1872. The society's eclipse no doubt owed something to the sudden death of Brotherton in March 1866, but the ready acquiescence of the remaining activists in the transfer of energies to the Manchester Education Bill Committee suggests the extent to which its fundamental purpose had been investigative, and its objectives were being achieved.[43] Through not only Brotherton's initial writings and the early reports of the society, but also via notable papers at the Society of Arts, and at the 1866 National Association for the Promotion of Social Science conference, the EAS had firmly established what H.A. Bruce, when introducing one of the forerunners of the 1870 Education Act in the Commons in 1867, described as the 'thunderclap from Manchester'.[44] By 1868, revelations of the educational 'disease' that investigations in Manchester had uncovered, had been promulgated by an educational conference in Manchester

in January, and widely acknowledged in the national press.[45] The political manoeuvrings which eventually brought success in Parliament were
tortuous, and were marked by the fracturing of the EAS constituency into
two camps supporting the contending positions of the National Education
League and the National Education Union. But they were ultimately
founded on the mobilisation and extension of local statistics,[46] cemented
by the parliamentary sponsored investigations of D.R. Fearon into working-
class education in a number of towns including Manchester. Fearon's report,
though it focused more on quality than quantity, endorsed the broad outline
of the EAS position. 'A short coercion bill for the restraint of statisticians is
evidently urgently needed', bristled Nunn.[47]

In fact, the 1870 Act was less restraining order than endowment, effectively enshrining the practice of local investigation through its stipulation
that new board schools were to be provided only in localities where existing
accommodation was manifestly deficient. The Manchester School Board
was forced to operate in its early years in a complex spatial field and its politics were dominated by conflicts of statistical geography.[48] Immediately on
establishment, the School Board undertook a comprehensive survey of the
city, which identified particular areas where there was a shortfall (predominantly in Hulme).[49] For Nunn, who became leader of the obstructionists to
extending board schooling, this was recognisably a question of statistical
method which he was prepared to challenge both in Manchester and elsewhere.[50] At one level, the approach of the school board became steadily
more Euclidian, in the sense that the question of educational deficiency
increasingly became a matter of arithmetic, based on the artificial registration districts and sub-districts, rather than the precise cartographic imaginaries of Brotherton.[51] In 1874, 'the whole city [was] mapped out by circles
of one-eighth of a mile radius, the centre of each circle being the exact
position of an existing or projected Protestant school', and this provided the
basis on which discussions about areas of deficiency proceeded.[52] At the
same time, the Board had to continue to wrestle with the actual social and
physical topographies, the difficulties of finding sites for schools in areas of
accommodation shortages, the need to understand the complex neighbourhood dynamics of class status or religion, which could disrupt purely geometric catchment areas.[53] The desired configuration constantly modulated
as the population shifted and provision ebbed and flowed. Through the first
decades of the Board's work there was a constant stream of local enquiries into deficiencies of accommodation in specific blocks and districts.[54]
Observers, including HM Inspectors, continued to recognise the importance
of geographic variation which made aggregate figures unhelpful.[55] Only
from chief inspectors' reports for the later 1880s and 1890s do we get some
sense of the decay of geographical imperatives, and a tendency to look at the
district as in some senses isotropic.[56]

The machinery of knowledge formation was transformed, but slowly. The appointment of school board attendance officers (SBVs) did not always mean a new corps of professional observers producing new information flows: in Ancoats the attendance officer of the Education Aid Society was reappointed under the Board.[57] Although it was suggested in the early 1870s that SBVs engaged in 'a system of personal examination of the various districts to which the population had been driven, or where the population had accumulated', School Board enquiries well into the 1880s remained remarkably rudimentary.[58] The population of districts was calculated by counting houses, and educational need might be assessed on the basis of a brief tour by the clerk to the Board.[59] In 1889, Fred Scott noted that his ambition to replicate Charles Booth's London survey in Manchester had been thwarted in part because the Manchester SBVs only collected information relating to families where the school fees were remitted.[60] Only gradually did the numbers of SBVs expand to a point at which they might have provided the sort of input Booth achieved in his London poverty surveys. From 1886 to 1894, the number increased from 18 to 27; even at this level, their role was primarily to assess parental ability to pay, visit absent scholars and undertake periodic special censuses to identify children of school age who had not yet commenced school. The evidence is contradictory, but it seems likely at this point that they didn't have all the school-age children in Manchester on their books.[61] Only in the final few years of the century was there rapid expansion to the 1900 figure of 50. By this point, the Board possessed an experienced cadre of officers, who not only dealt with irregular attendance, but also investigated applications for exemption, ensured that all cases of infectious disease were reported to the Medical Officer of Health, reported weekly to the Guardians of those in families in receipt of relief and also advised the Board on all those living in 'vicious surroundings'.[62]

The example of the local efforts to extend education in Manchester offers an illuminating parallel to the histories of sanitary reform in the Victorian period explored in recent scholarship. In both cases, social knowledge was created by the traditional amalgam of religious, philanthropic and professional elites, aligned with rather than operating against visiting associations, drawing on the practices of house-to-house engagement and the expertise of active visitors to construct a self-consciously statistical discourse which was concrete, historicised, geographically specific and acutely aware of the opacity of urban space.

Notes

1 As the *MG* noted in an editorial, 11 November 1846, citing an article in the *British Quarterly*, this was one argument that opponents of a national system of education were likely to avoid.

2 See, for example, the observations of the Manchester Church Education Society in its (1st to 5th) *Annual Reports* (1845–9).

3 Evidence of George Hull Bowers, *Select Committee on Education in Manchester and Salford. First Report, PP* (1852) XI, 202. The problem was reiterated in the reports of the education inspectors, for example the report of HMI Frederick Watkin, which singled out the parishes of St George's, St Andrew's and Holy Trinity, Hulme as districts where the rapid increase in population was far outstripping the supply of schooling, *Committee of Council on Education. Report, PP* (1847), XLV, 223. See Charles Richson, *Education in Manchester. Considered with Special Reference to the State of Church Day Schools and the Means of Extending Education Generally* (1850), e.g. 4–5. See the winding up of the Congregational Education Society, *MG*, 29 August 1846.

4 Report of W.J. Kennedy, *Committee of Council on Education. Report, PP* (1850), XLIII, 145–7, which included comments such as 'rather too much scolding … but the district is a very poor and rough one', 145.

5 Note the limits to the geographical debate; so Richson's *Educational Facts and Statistics of Manchester* (1852) focused entirely on figures at the level of 'Manchester and Salford' combined; his evidence to the *Select Committee on Education in Manchester and Salford. First Report* did address distribution more explicitly, but by operating at the level at and even above registration district, he was able to 'demonstrate' that schooling was especially provided in districts which had the largest proportion of the poor; see Q105–115, 160–73.

6 John Watts, *MX*, 8 February 1851; compare with the enquiry launched in 1847 on the 'unevenness of educational provision'; the agent employed gave a report on conditions in Ancoats, *MC*, 30 October 1847; LPSA *Plan* (1847). The NPSA scheme involved not just school districts, but also the employment of 'visitors' (Watts indicated that these might be existing town or city missioners, or others employed specifically for the role) who would ascertain the exact level of destitute children in their district. Watts evidence to the *Select Committee on Education in Manchester and Salford. Second Report, PP* (1852–3) XXIV, Q827. For evidence that this perception was also a feature of voluntarist responses to the education question, see the comments of James Sidebottom, *MG*, 27 September 1851.

7 See *Select Committee on Education in Manchester and Salford. First Report, PP* (1852) XI, evidence of Richson, Q325–327.

8 *MG*, 10 January 1857, *Manchester Weekly Advertiser* (hereafter *MWA*), 29 December 1860.

9 'Statistics of Education in Manchester and Salford', Edward Brotherton Scrapbook, M98/2, Manchester Archives.

10 See Watts evidence to the *Select Committee on Education in Manchester and Salford. Second Report, PP* (1852–3) XXIV, Q527.

11 *MC*, 30 October 1847, followed up by newspaper correspondence on conditions in particular districts, *MG*, 1 November 1848; John Watts, *Report*. See the survey of William Birley, reported in *MG*, 3 April 1850, and Charles Richson, *A Sketch of Some of the Causes which, in Manchester, Induced the Abandonment of the Voluntary System in Support of Schools, and the Introduction of the Manchester and Salford Education Bill* (1851), 47–50.

12 J. McCartie's survey of St Jude's in 1858, *MG*, 4 July 1859; which was used to contribute to the debate on educational provision in the following decade, *MC*, 25 March 1865.

13 *Select Committee on Education in Manchester and Salford. First Report, PP* (1852) XI, evidence of Richson, Q309, with it reference to house-to-house visits to enquire into reasons for absence from school; in total involving visits to 17,426 families in poorer districts. Also reference to a separate inquiry into 26 poorer districts by agents under the supervision of Mr Minchin (Q334); these were cross-referenced to police evidence of the proportion of inhabitants known to them, and also to Poor Law data about the proportions known to have been at one time in receipt of poor relief.

14 For the use made of this sort of information, see the discussion in 'On the Social Condition of the Working Classes of Manchester', *MX*, 18 February 1852.

15 See comments of William Morris, *MX*, 10 January 1857; ditto James Collinge, who spoke of the palpable want of school accommodation in both St George's (500 for a parish of 20,000) and St Paul's (200 for a parish of 8,000). The problem had existed for a long time, Collinge argued, and it was about time it was dealt with, *MWA*, 29 December 1860; *MG*, 19 January 1861.

16 See the riposte of Brotherton, *MG*, 16 July 1864. (As the *MG* had commented in an editorial on the 14 July, Kennedy's position was in essentials obviously different from that of the Education Aid Society in any case.) Gradually, Kennedy was drawn into the society's orbit, appearing on the EAS platform, and by 1870 his position – that an educational relieving officer was all that was really needed to solve the educational problem – was largely indistinguishable from the Society's, see EAS *Report* for 1870, as extracted in *MG*, 23 July 1870.

17 See Rumney on 'Compulsory Education', in *Report of the First Meeting of Members of the National Education League* (1869), 108–22.

18 McKerrow, citing material from the *MCMMag*, Q320; Watts citing Layhe, Q527, *Select Committee on Education in Manchester and Salford. Second Report, PP* (1852–3) XXIV (and also suggesting that Manchester City missionaries might be used as school attendance officers under a system of rate-supported schools, see Q827).

19 Evidence of Adshead, *Select Committee on Education in Manchester and Salford. First Report, PP* (1852) XI, Q2027.

20 This was established without public fanfare by Le Mare: support was offered to help the poorest of the working class to meet educational expenditure, and visitors (these might have been the regular MCM city missionaries) were employed in working-class districts to encourage attendance. By 1857, it was supporting 3,000 children. See *MCMMag* (May 1854), 100–1, (May 1855), 8, and Kay-Shuttleworth, *Four Periods*, 115–16; a similar society was noted earlier *MCMMag* (February 1853), 8; for a further reference see W.J. Kennedy, 'On the Principles to be Observed in Schemes Promoting School Attendance', in A Hill, ed., *Essays Upon Educational Subjects* (1857), 226–39.

21 Brotherton, *Popular Education in Manchester and Salford* (1864), *idem, Popular Education and Political Economy* (1865).

22 Brotherton, *Popular Education*, 11–12.

23 See, for example, the discussion in David Englander, 'Comparisons and Contrasts: Henry Mayhew and Charles Booth as Social Investigators', in Englander and O'Day, *Riches*, 105–42, 117.

24 See the contribution of Brotherton, *MG*, 21 December 1864.

25 J.A. Bremner, 'By what means can the impediments to the Education of Children of the Manual-Labour class, arising from the apathy or poverty of Parents, and the Claims of the Market for Labour, be most effectually removed', *Transactions*

of the National Association for the Promotion of Social Science (1866), 307–17, quote at 307.

26   Brotherton, *Popular Education and Political Economy*, 31.

27   See the slips in Brotherton Scrapbook, M98/297, Manchester Archives; see the extended vignette in *MG*, 15 February 1866.

28   Education Aid Society, *Annual Reports* (1865–7); *MG*, 6 March 1865. For a study of the work of the society, see Henry Roper, 'Toward an Elementary Education Act for England and Wales, 1865–68', *British Journal of Educational Studies* 23 (1975), 181–208.

29   J.A. Bremner 'On the Principle of Compulsion in Primary Education', *TMSS* (1869–70), 38. For the schools survey see *MG*, 13 March 1866, EAS, *Annual Report* (1867), 13–17. This activity continued alongside regular contacts with the city's schools, see note of the visit of Watts to St Michael's school, Hulme, M65/18/5/1, minutes 27 Sept 1865, Manchester Archives.

30   See Brotherton, *Popular Education and Political Economy*, 7–9, 28.

31   Oats, 'Deansgate', 1–13; Henry C. Oats, 'Inquiry into the Educational and Other Conditions of a District in Ancoats, *Transactions of the Manchester Statistical Society* (1865–6), 1–16; T.R. Wilkinson, 'Report on the Educational and Other Conditions of a District at Gaythorn and Knott Mill, Manchester, Visited in January 1868, with Observations Suggested by the Visitation', *TMSS* (1867–8), 53–78. For Brotherton's comment see letter, *MG* (dating from the start of December 1864), Brotherton Scrapbook, M98/126, MA.

32   Crook, *Governing Systems*, 98.

33   See his intervention 'correcting EB's statistics', *MG*, 2 December 1865, *MG*, 8 December 1865.

34   Letter of Nunn, *MG*, 18 January 1864.

35   *MC*, 8 January 1866, responding to Brotherton, *MC*, 21 December 1865, John S. Mayson, *MC*, 30 December 1865, 4 January 1866. See also the recollection of Watts, *MCN*, 31 October 1885. Instead, Nunn argued conveniently that knowledge of the educational condition of the working classes in the parish 'must be arrived at indirectly, by constant intercourse with them, by taking particulars in a sufficient number of instances and by inferring from them the state of the whole'.

36   Letter, *MC*, 16 February 1867.

37   Brotherton Scrapbook, M98/298, Manchester Archives.

38   Richson, 'On the Fallacies Involved in Certain Parliamentary Returns of Day Schools and Scholars, in England and Wales, in 1818, 1833, & 1851', *TMSS* (1853), 1–16. Kay-Shuttleworth paid tribute to Richson's 'statistical experience', in his *Four Periods*, 101.

39   Evidence of Adshead, *Select Committee on Education in Manchester and Salford. First Report*, *PP* (1852) XI, Q2027.

40   EAS, *Annual Report* (1865), 7. It was also noted that the data had never been drawn from the very worst districts, because these had initially been avoided as below the reach of the society's work.

41   See Joseph Nunn, *Facts and Fallacies on the Condition of Popular Education in Manchester, with Reference to the New Education Bill* [1866], 13, where the distribution argument is used to refute Brotherton's suggestions of general insufficiency of provision.

42   EAS, *Annual Report* (1866), 7, *Annual Report* (1867), 10, 12. The evidence of the surveys indicated that nearly half the elder siblings could not read or write.

43 The Manchester Education Bill Committee was chaired by the prominent Liberal Francis Taylor, and its leading supporters included Benjamin Armitage, Watts, Mayson, Bremner, Herbert Philips and others, see S.E. Maltby, *Manchester and the Movement for National Elementary Education, 1800–1870* (1918), 105–20.

44 For details, see Roper, 'Toward an Elementary Education Act', and Maltby, *Manchester and National Education*; the discussion at the Society of Arts is detailed in *Journal of the Society of Arts* XV (1866–7), 515–17, at the National Association for the Promotion of Social Science in Bremner, 'Impediments to the Education of Children', 307–17. For the kind of widespread press coverage obtained, see, for example, *Ragged School Union Magazine* XVIII (1866), 37, itself citing the *Educational Record*.

45 See editorials, *Western Daily Press*, 17 January 1868, *Daily News*, 18 January, 26 May 1868, quoted in *MG*, 27 May 1868, *Liverpool Mercury*, 18 January 1868, *London Evening Standard*, 23 January 1868.

46 See *The Times*, 13 October 1869; compare Watts' role in the deputation to the prime minister, *MC*, 11 March 1868.

47 See Joseph Nunn, *Strictures on the Reports on Education in Manchester, Liverpool, Birmingham and Leeds, Presented to the House of Commons by Messrs J.G. Fitch and D.R. Fearon etc ... Addressed to the Rt Hon W.E. Forster* (1870), 9; letter, *MCN*, 19 March 1870; also 17 September 1870.

48 J. Watts, *Work of the First Manchester School Board* (1873).

49 See Manchester School Board Minutes, M65/1/1/1/147-48, Manchester Archives. The survey, which returned results by registration district, identified 5 in Manchester with a notional surplus accommodation, but also 5 with deficiencies, a modest 400 in Market Street, but nearly 1,500 in Ardwick and as much as 2,000 in Chorlton.

50 See letters to *School Board Chronicle*, 21 September 1872, 4 June, 4 September, 16 October 1875. An article entitled 'A Question of Statistics', *School Board Chronicle*, 9 October 1875, 358, reviewed the discussion and came down against Nunn.

51 For example, *MCN*, 2 May 1874; see discussion *MCN*, 25 December 1875.

52 W. Bremner, *School Board Work in Manchester* (1874) (as reviewed by *School Board Chronicle*, 10 October 1874). The *School Board Triennial Report* for 1890 presented a map of 161 elementary schools in Manchester, including accommodation provided to demonstrate that full coverage had been achieved.

53 See the account of the debate in School Board, *MCN*, 29 June 1872. For the problems of having to accept cramped and unsuitable sites in the early years, see the case of the Ardwick Street Board School, Manchester School Board Papers, M65/1/93/69-70, Manchester Archives, and the earlier comments of the Kennedy's report on the All Saints district in 1856,

54 See, for example, School Board Papers, M65/1/93/139, Manchester Archives. It was not just about whether districts with insufficient provision could be identified, but whether in some instances the pattern of provision resulted in obstacles for some potential scholars where the existing schools nearest were unwilling to take them because of their social background.

55 'General Report for the Year 1883 by Her Majesty's Inspector H.E. Oakeley on the Schools Inspected in the Manchester District', *Committee of Council on Education: Report, PP* (1884) XXIV 348–9.

56 It did not stop Crosfield rehearsing similar rhetorics in calling for free schools in 1891 (though defeated), *MCN*, 31 January 1891.

57 See 'School Board Work in Manchester', *MCN*, 29 March 1873. For a revealing study of the London experience, see David Rubinstein, *School Attendance in London, 1870–1914: A Social History* (1969), 42–53.

58 William Hughes, 'On Elementary Education', *TMSS* (1875–6), 35. For the attendance officers, see for example, 'A Walk with the School Board Officer', *Manchester Guardian*, 17 September 1873. In the early years, their activities were restricted by the unwillingness of the board to vigorously prosecute the parents of children who were not making the numbers of attendances required by the by-law (allowing all who made 50% attendances to remain unpursued), see the debate in School Board, *MCN*, 26 December 1874; this was raised to 80% in April 1875 when statistics were published showing that if anything total attendance had fallen away, *MCN*, 1 May 1875. This is turn prompted the resumption of 'street raids', *MCN*, 27 March 1875; *MCN*, 1 May 1880. Angel Meadow, *MCN*, 3 November 1885.

59 School Board Sites Committee Minutes, M65/19/5/115, /147-49, School Board Papers, Manchester Archives.

60 Scott, 'Condition and Occupations', 93–4.

61 *School Board Triennial Reports* (1891–4), 7–8, compared with Watts, 'Fifteen Years', 89.

62 'Phases of School Board Work: Afternoon with an Attendance Officer', *MCN*, 4 December 1897; in which the SBV is reported to claim that 'he practically knows the history of every family in his district, and much more intimately than the district visitor, the clergyman, or the policeman', *MCN*, 28 September 1901.

6   Conclusion

Late nineteenth-century decay

The visiting mode and its consequences endured well beyond the end of the Victorian period, visible in a range of twentieth-century health and social services.[1] However, challenges to its pre-eminence as a source of social knowledge are visible from the 1870s, in the expansion of the statistical endeavours of the central state[2] and in the more varied modes associated with the practices of 'slumming' and the settlement movement. Nevertheless, visiting societies continued to occupy a central place in the knowledge economy, and much of the extended range of social activities, including the important ragged school and mission hall movements of the later century, were closely aligned to the established visiting institutions and absorbed most of their assumptions and approaches.[3] Visiting institutions, old and new, were still the basis for much reportage.[4] The house-to-house inquiry remained the gold standard for obtaining both social knowledge and the authority to speak on it.[5] The group of social commentators who came to prominence in Manchester in the last years of the century, Alexander Forrest, C.E.B. Russell, Charles Rowley, Gilbert Kirlew, continued to draw their knowledge and standing from the same sorts of backgrounds in visiting-inflected philanthropy common to their predecessors.[6] The reliance placed by James Niven as MOH on information gathered by the district visitors of the Ladies Sanitary Association, and the willingness of the corporation to pay a steadily increasing number of them in the 1890s is a mark of the transitional nature of the period.[7] There was a steady decline in the sense that working areas were beyond knowledge and influence, as they increasingly seem to be colonised by institutions and more fully supervised by the police, attendance officers and municipal officials.[8] The visiting mode was being replaced by an 'inspection' mode,[9] just as philanthropic solutions at the local level were being superseded by national legislative responses.

Until the early twentieth century, at which point shifts of emphasis are more visible, these institutions continued to operate within understandings of 'spatial pathology', albeit of an evolving sort. One shift was a movement in the centre of gravity from the home to the street associated on the one hand with problems of young adolescents, and on the other with the emergence of the flâneur as a distinct literary type.[10] This was visible by the later 1870s in association with the developing activities of the school board officers (SBVs), whose programme of 'raids' was often presented as dealing with 'street children' or the 'street Arab' and the problem of 'rowdyism'.[11] This shift was reflected in the Manchester-based social literature of the period, most obviously in Hesba Stretton's *Pilgrim Street*, but also in the publications of Alfred Alsop and the Wood Street Mission, including *From Light to Darkness; or Voices from the Slums* (1881).[12] This was still a geographic denomination, and one in which an ostensible shift in attention to the street and the wanderer shouldn't be allowed to mask the persistent reliance on domestic encounters.[13] There was little of the aimlessness and the emphasis on movement through rather than arrival at which characterises the 'excursion mode' of Walter Benjamin. This is also true of the second development, the settlement movement of the 1890s.[14] In some respects, the push for settlement houses marked an intensification of spatial anxieties, a sense that '[a] great deal of the worst distress is unknown even to mission workers in the slums',[15] and that 'it is not possible to get a full knowledge of the life of the poor unless one's whole life is spent in their midst'.[16] This had the potential to intensify territorialisation, and often involved an enrichment of visiting rather than its replacement,[17] but it also involved attention to a wider range of phenomena, including for example unemployment, and a shift from ideas of learning *about* to notions of learning *with* or even *from* which undermined the observational imperative of the visiting mode.[18]

The settlement movement was associated with the extension of forms of expert knowledge and the growth of state bureaucracies encouraged by the coalescence of social work as a recognised specialism in the Edwardian period.[19] By the mid-1900s, lectures on social work were being delivered in Manchester at the Ancoats University Settlement,[20] and from 1907 the Manchester League of Help offered a version of social aid that combined visitation with the functions of an incipient citizens' advice bureau. The development of an approach based on case files provided direct, as opposed to indirect, biographical information, and so rendered judgements on the state of houses largely irrelevant. Indeed, the League of Help files, while collecting information about health, employment, rental and family circumstances, did not specifically collect information about the state of the home. There was a greater willingness to engage in explicit longitudinal investigation of life histories. This was particularly visible in the sustained debate in the 1890s about the prevalence of 'hereditary pauperism'.[21] It might also be argued that there was a significant shift in the final decades of the century towards the supersession of local organised philanthropy by larger, geographically unspecific city-wide philanthropy.

The crisis of the late Victorian economy, with its intensification of industrial conflict, created a dramatic increase in interest in data on unemployment, industrial welfare and economic relations.[22] Gradually, under the influence of the Labour Bureau and legislation like the Factories and Workshops Act (1901), greater attention was given to the occupational determinants of health.[23] This was evident in John Tatham's pioneering exploration of the relative mortality of different occupations, although this was initially pursued through the examination of specific districts as concentrations of specific occupations. Occupation was very much the focus of Niven as Manchester's Medical Officer of Health after 1900 (visible, for example, in the occupational focus of the data collected in his 1908 morbidity inquiry in St John's ward).[24] Likewise, the shift in public health from zymotic approaches towards a focus on the specific vectors of the transmission and development of disease, not only emphasised the environmental and structural causes of poverty, but also shifted attention from specific 'fever nests' to the broader ecology of morbidity.[25] The 1898 Report of the Royal Commission on Tuberculosis which provided incontrovertible evidence of the transmission of tuberculosis through infected milk, produced particularly prompt action in Manchester, such as the Manchester Milk Clauses Act (1899), and the subsequent construction of what Anne Hardy has described as a new regime of 'municipal veterinary hygiene.[26]

Into the 1890s, social reform movements in the localities continued to focus on housing. Graham Mooney has outlined the ways in which Manchester was at the forefront of research into disinfection in the late-Victorian period; if this encouraged a move to the laboratory and the experiment, it also continued to emphasise the domestic; the Manchester bacteriologist Sheridan Delepine operated in a specially constructed space he likened to 'an ordinary living room'.[27] Similarly, Manchester continued to be recognised as leading the way in the promulgation of sanitary education through local visiting and tract distribution.[28] Hence the development under the auspices of the M&SSA of the Working Men's Health Homes Societies, or the activities of the Social Questions Union's 'conditions of home life committee', which produced major initiatives such as T.R. Marr's 1904 survey, which picks up Niven's call for a detailed house-to-house investigation in one of Manchester's sanitary districts, to call for a comprehensive house-to-house survey.[29] (So much so that Joyce can talk about a shift from the street to the house at the end of the Victorian period.[30]) John Saunders, the organising agent of the Hulme Healthy

Homes Society noted that 'Our formula was to go right to the people, to their very doors'.[31] But in the light of the evidence emerging from, for example, the 1885 Royal Commission on Housing, of the underlying structural forces operating on residential patterns, housing shifted from cause to symptom, and from an index of capacity to an agency of deterioration in its own right.[32] The mid-1890s saw the peak of fin-de-siècle slum clearance; there is a sense thereafter that it was increasingly a technical problem.[33] The shift to environmentalism was facilitated (but it was also obscured) by the fact that it shared much with the previous knowledge regime, and especially its linkage of home and character, simply reversing the causal vectors so that debased homes created debased populations, rather than vice versa.

These changes are registered above all in a number of linguistic shifts, such as the move from 'dwellings' (and to lesser degree 'homes') to 'houses' visible between Samelson's *Dwellings and the Death Rate in Manchester* (1883) and the reports on housing of the early 1900s.[34] The prevalent language of the slums began to generalise and consolidate the various districts. Ancoats with its specific sub-districts was displaced in the popular consciousness by the broader, less differentiated and also less philanthropically colonised mass of Hulme.[35] The increasing 'anonymisation' of districts allowed them to function primarily as representative of broader problems. The sense of particularity of place which was at the heart of the cartographic imagination did not disappear. Indeed, despite the massifying rhetoric, there was still a great deal of coverage based on the identification of the specific characteristics of particular locales.[36] But it was certainly diluted.[37]

Housing discussions at the turn of the century were marked by much greater use of standardised classifications, such as measurements of the numbers of people per room, or the numbers of rooms per house, taking equal numbers of rooms as providing sufficient equivalence for the figures to make sense, than had previously been the case.[38] This can be set alongside the use of new forms of data; for instance, the sort of anthropometric data on heights used in evidence to the 1904 Interdepartmental Enquiry into Physical Deterioration; and previously e.g. by Howson Ray, Salford's Medical Officer of Health around 1900,[39] and the intrusion of novel statistical methods, including discussions like Tatham's *Manchester Life Table* (1892) which dispensed with attempts at mapping, and treated the population as de-spatialised.[40] In general by 1900, aided by the strengthening of the academic deployment of statistics, there was a greater willingness to engage in complex mathematical manipulation and modelling as part of a more 'scientific', quantitatively sophisticated engagement with data which marks Niven's work as MOH in the 1890s.[41]

However, as several recent histories have emphasised, this process was slow and uncertain, and many of these developments were only visible at the very end of the century. So there was no compulsory infectious disease notification until 1889 (as an opt in – but one largely taken up in provincial towns) and 1899 (as mandatory), despite the long-standing campaigning of Ransome and the creation of a voluntary system in Manchester as early as 1860.[42] If there is any transitional moment it would seem to be between Charles Booth's London investigations in the 1880s (which in their essentially subjective classification system clearly operated within the central assumptions and practices of the visiting mode) and World War I. Rowntree's study of York with its systematic attempt to estimate household income marks something of a half-way house.[43]

Conclusion

In his 1995 essay on Booth's *Life and Labour*, David Reeder, in asking why Booth chose to adopt a spatial approach to the presentation of social data, suggested that little is known about the reasons for this choice.[44] The argument here is that the basis of Booth's approach was neither opaque nor unusual; rather, he was merely adopting and developing both a method and a conception deeply entrenched in the practice of Victorian social investigation. Not merely in his emphasis on the spatial analysis of social problems, but also his use of 'visitors' to collect data, his mapping of social strata largely on the basis of housing type and condition and his attempts to provide what David Englander describes as a 'photographic' rendition of social conditions, all place Booth at the culmination of a long-established set of practices.[45]

This was not the only method of social knowing, of course. The 'visiting' mode approaches discussed here operated alongside an extensive and extending system of quantitative information generation propagated locally by individuals such as David Chadwick, perhaps the only local statistician operating consistently outside the visiting mode in the mid-Victorian decades,[46] and nationally by figures such as William Farr, John Simon and the activities of the General Registry Office, which often aligned closely with massifying notions. Farr, for example, spoke of aggregate mortality figures as a mechanism by which individuals 'divested of all colour, form, character, passion and the infinite individualities of life; by abstraction … are reduced to mere units'.[47] Equally, social arithmetic, counting and summing, remained a fundamental component of the rhetorics by which institutions, including visiting institutions, described and justified their own activities. It is not a case of the 'failure' of social investigation against some scientific standard, of a trough before Booth put English sociology back on the right track, but of recognising the nature of social knowledge as it was in this period, a mix of prison statistics, memoirs of workers, impressionistic 'urban exploration' literature, accounts of philanthropic work and papers from the National Association for the Promotion of Social Science.

Reeder's puzzlements speak to the extent to which dominant versions of the history of nineteenth-century social statistics and social action more generally have systematically misconceived the fundamental impulses of mid-Victorian social investigation, even as they have recognised that Booth's survey 'vividly reminded its readers that the city was made up of individuals within households and not impersonal averages or wholes. The authority of the survey rested not only on its claim to scientific objectivity and comprehensiveness, but upon its specificity and particularity'.[48] The traditional narrative of a burst of statistical and survey work which dies out around 1850 not to be actively renewed until around 1890 cannot be sustained once the limits of the statistical revolution at the local level and its continuities after 1850 are recognised.[49] Social investigation was tied more closely to reforming or philanthropic agendas than was perhaps desirable, but it did not disappear, or even substantially decay, both in the traditions of urban criticism represented by the writings of figures like Thomas Wright, Hector Gavin and George Sims, as well as in the more quantitative analyses of Booth and Rowntree.[50] We need to escape from a version of social knowledge which unduly concentrates on the state apparatus, and which explicitly or implicitly relegates alternative approaches to the status of survivals or resistances: the introduction of a new way of seeing does not mean the diminution and eventual disappearance of older ways.[51]

In the same way, the long-standing resistance to sampling, and the painstakingly slow adoption of European techniques of mathematical statistics, the error curve, variance and distribution difference, even after the early work of Galton and Pearson, which has most recently concerned Schweber, seems less unaccountable once the blockage to the acceptance of abstracted populations produced by the dominant territorialisation of knowledge in nineteenth-century Britain is recognised.[52]

In this sense, for all the sharpness of its insights and the fruitfulness of the questions raised by the existing scholarship, the material presented here suggests the need for a wholesale rethinking of a body of scholarship stretching across social and cultural history, gender and literary studies, and historical geography which has offered an unsustainably categoric view of the operations of nineteenth-century institutions of surveillance and reformation, falling too readily into a discussion of purpose and ambition, rather than getting caught up with the much messier questions of actual realisation. We need to take up the challenge to go beyond fantasies of panoptic power to look at the actualities of spatial practices posed among others by

Ian Hacking, and place visitors alongside engineers, architects and statisticians among the nineteenth century's 'technicians of space'.[53]

It can be argued that more recent work has already substantially challenged the dominant Foucauldian paradigm, drawing attention to the resources of resistance to omniscient state authority. Yet, mostly what has been achieved is merely to shift existing judgements of the balance between power and resistance back in favour of the latter, and a move from the Foucault of *Discipline and Punish* to the Foucault of 'governmentality'.[54] Greater weight is given to the limits of totalising forces, and to their dispersal, but they remain at the heart of the analysis, the realities against which they engage constructed as barrier or obstacle. At the same time, the suggestion has been made that the limits of the early Victorian 'statistical revolution' rested primarily on the survival of older models of disinterest based on aristocratic codes of public service. The analysis offered here seeks to go significantly further by arguing for an understanding based on alternatives rather than adjustments, and of essentially nineteenth-century modes of knowledge rather than merely a repackaged *noblesse oblige*.[55] It was not merely that Foucauldian mechanisms of knowledge/power were partial, but that they were not paradigmatic. Victorian urban knowledge regimes were – perhaps not wholly but very significantly – based on models deriving not from the disciplinary state, nor from aristocratic gentility, but from reforming urban voluntarism, on technologies not of inspection but of visiting, on classificatory regimes which were as much narratological as phenomenological. Above all, and for all these reasons, social knowledge in Victorian Britain was spatial and situated. It was not primarily that imperatives of abstraction and omniscience were compromised, nor that they were fiercely contested by Victorian cultural criticism, but rather that until the final few years of the period they were marginal.

To existing arguments about the enduring prevalence of voluntarism, I contribute here the significance of the visiting mode as a technology of knowledge, and the particular forms of territorial understanding it produced. The 'visiting mode', which cannot be defined by gender, be belittled as the officious intrusiveness of a Mrs Pardiggle or a nuisance inspector, or rendered as merely subordinate or epiphenomenal to central totalising apparatus, warns us of the dangers of the 'reductive universalization' of Foucault's connections of space and power, of the tendency to render all resistance to the creation of transparent geometric space as both residual and ultimately nugatory.[56] It reaffirms that efforts of mapping in the nineteenth century, especially its cartographic imaginaries, neither manufactured power nor created a spatial panopticon.[57] Against the liberal governmentality of Joyce and others, we must oppose what de Certeau calls 'the opaque, blind domain of the inhabited city'.[58]

Without doubt, the 1830s and 1840s see a peculiarly Victorian 'liberal' regime of knowledge emerging out of a number of institutions and practices, including mapping and statistics, which sought to know the city but which also emphasised the obscurity of the working classes and their habitations. These approaches co-opted but they did not supersede the distinctive modes of investigation and understanding that we can designate the nineteenth-century 'visiting mode'. The traditional authority of groups such as clergy-men and philanthropists persisted and was reinforced by its collaborations with the emerging cadres of disinterested experts. Central to the intellectual or ideological work of these institutions and practices was the rendering of the working classes as agential and mobile, and hence a concern with characterisation rather than classification. The consequence was an understanding of society based on (what we might describe as) 'biographical metonymies', not least housing, and a particular statistical moment in which the concept of 'distribution' was geographical, not arithmetical. Far from the abstract, geometric, two-dimensional thinness of the Foucauldian perspective, social knowledge was material, morphological and multidimensional. In the nineteenth century, enplotment thickened.

Notes

1 See Heggie, 'Health Visiting and District Nursing in Victorian Manchester', 403–22; Becky Taylor and Ben Rogaly, '"Mrs Fairly is a Dirty, Lazy Type": Unsatisfactory Households and the Problem of Problem Families, Norwich 1942 to 1963', *Twentieth Century British History* 18 (2007), 429–52.

2 Roger Davidson, *Whitehall and the Labour Problem in Late Victorian and Edwardian Britain. A Study in Official Statistics and Social Control* (1985).

3 *MCN*, 17 April 1886. See, for example, comments of the *Unitarian Herald* on the Manchester Domestic Mission, 30 April 1886: 'The philanthropist, the social reformer, the sanitary philosopher, the religious teacher, will find in these records facts and inferences, statistics and results, which, from equally modest and trustworthy sources, are nowhere else supplied'; extensive extracts of the report were then published, 15 May 1886. For slumming, see Koven, *Slumming*; for Dowling, quoted 22, 'the 1870s and 80s were "the heyday of slumming as social regulation"'. For the continuities of the history of philanthropy and ragged schools and mission halls, see the comments on mission halls in J.W. MacGill, in *The Christian Worker* VII (1886), 12, and the histories of individual ragged schools, including John-st Pendleton, Heyrod-st, Charter Street, Poland St, Old Garret Ragged School, McCormack Street Ragged School and Mission. (Note that in Ancoats in the mid-1890s, before the Ancoats settlement, these included the work of the Crossleys at the Star Hall, Every St, the Heyrod-st Ragged School and Working People's Institute, the Holland-Street Ragged School, the Every Street Congregational Mission and the Central Wesleyan Mission Hall, see, *MG*, 5 February 1895; others appearing around here include the George Street Sunday School and Mission, Ancoats (*MG*, 14 December 1897).

4　See 'A Days Round with the Sanitary Woman', *MCN*, 4 November 1893; as well as extracts from the annual report of the Ladies Sanitary Association, *MCN*, 16 May 1891, articles in *MG*, 18 January 1898, *MCN*, 3 December 1892.

5　See, for example, the letter of Alexander Forrest, *MG*, 19 January 1886; Alexander Forrest, who was a regular contributor to the local press on social topics in the 1880s and 1890s, had been Hon. Secretary of the Holt Town Ragged School in the 1860s and 1870s.

6　Gilbert Kirlew, Secretary of the Strangeways Boys and Girls Refuge, started as a Methodist tract distributor, and then for several years was a worker at the Heyrod-st Ragged School, see E.W. Kirlew, *Gilbert R Kirlew. A Memoir* (1908), see *Revival Times*, 7 February 1908. Although these philanthropic workers were not especially active in the monthly meetings of the MSS in this period, they did still contribute, as for example in Gilbert R. Kirlew, 'Facts and Figures Relating to Street Children', *TMSS* (1888–9), 43–50; likewise his paper to the Church Congress 1885. In the later 1890s, Kirlew was embroiled in a sexual abuse scandal, see Dean Pavlakis, 'Reputation and the Sexual Abuse of Boys: Changing Norms in Late-Nineteenth-Century Britain', *Men and Masculinities* 17.3 (2014), 231–52.

7　Schweber, *Disciplining Statistics*, 193–4. See comments on investigation into infant feeding in *MOH Report for 1897–98*, 270–5. Vanessa Heggie, 'Lies, Damn Lies, and Manchester's Recruiting Statistics: Degeneration as an "Urban Legend" in Victorian and Edwardian Britain', *Journal of the History of Medicine and Allied Sciences* 63.2 (2008), 178–216.

8　In respect of Charter-st Ragged School, it was noted that 'although poverty is still the badge of all who there reside, it is no longer unsafe for strangers to venture into its precincts', *MG*, 1 January 1884. For the shift from Booth to Rowntree, see E.P. Hennock, 'Concepts of Poverty in British Social Surveys from Charles Booth to Arthur Bowley', in M. Bulmer, ed., *The Social Survey in Historical Perspective* (1991); also Catherine Marsh, 'Informants, Respondents and Citizens', on the shift from informant to respondent modes.

9　The interesting distinction made in M. Valverde, 'The Dialectic of the Familiar and the Unfamiliar: The "Jungle" in Early Slum Travel Writing', *Sociology* 30 (1996), 507.

10　This is so notwithstanding the arguments of Walkowitz, *City of Dreadful Delight*, and Deborah Epstein Nord, *Walking the Victorian Streets. Women, Representation and the City* (1995); especially 'The Female Social Investigator: Maternalism, Feminism and Women's Work', 207–36.

11　*MCN*, 5, 12 January, 16 March 1878.

12　With its echoes in late-Victorian literature more generally; for example, works like Henry James's *The Princess Cassamassima*, which James said in his Preface to the New York edition 'proceeded … from the habit and the interest of walking the streets', quoted Schulling, *Dirt in Victorian Literature and Culture*, 131.

13　For a typical example, see 'Hard Times in Cottonopolis', *All The Year Round*, 17 May 1879, for which the author 'spent the whole of that day in visiting … some of the most destitute streets, lanes and courts of Manchester' but where he 'had talked in one denuded house after another with a score of haggard and almost hopeless men'.

14　M.E. Rose, 'The Manchester University Settlement in Ancoats, 1895–1909', *Manchester Region History Review* 7 (1993), 55–62, *idem*, 'Settlement of University Men in Great Towns: University Settlements in Manchester and

Liverpool', *Transactions of the Historic Society of Lancashire and Cheshire* 139 (1990), 137–60. For earlier articulations, see A Workman, 'A Voice from the Slums of Ancoats', *MCN*, 4 December 1886. It is possible to get some sense of this shift in Mayne, *Imagined Slums*. See not only the University Settlement and the Lancashire Independent College settlement, but also one conducted by Grosvenor Square Presbyterian Church, Hulme.

15 *MCN*, 20 February 1904.

16 Councillor James Johnston in *Report ... Housing of Poor*, 20. Compare with the comment by 'An Investigator', 'The Life of Some of the Poor: The Manchester Enquiry', *MG*, 7 April 1902, that information provided by health inspectors, police and district visitors is not enough. An examination of conditions requires residence; 'you must live among the poor and with them before you can speak with any authority' notes the author.

17 As in the defence of the Methodist Central Mission made by Dr Henry J. Pope in 1896, that its ministers had that ability to speak heart to heart to the working classes with the sort of 'illustrations taken from common life' made possible by 'diligent pastoral visitation', *MCN*, 18 January 1896.

18 For one unemployment survey see *MCN*, 2 February 1904. The new two-way process, traced by Bill Luckin in the 1930s, was clearly underway three decades earlier in the studies of unemployment in Manchester in 1904 undertaken by the Ancoats University Settlement and the Lancashire College Settlement (Hulme, assisted by the Grosvenor Square Presbyterian Church, All Saints, in another area of 'darkest Hulme'), a block of 58 streets between Oxford-st and Lower Medlock-st, where one out of every three houses visited contained at least one person out of work. See Bill Luckin, 'Revisiting the Slums in Manchester and Salford in the 1930s', in B. Doyle, ed., *Urban Politics and Space in the Nineteenth and Twentieth Centuries: Regional Perspectives* (2007), 134–47; letter of Charles Rowley, *MG*, 2 February 1895.

19 See Yeo, *Contest for Social Science*, 217–20. For Schweber, around 1885 was a terminal point because 'In England, a revival of partisan politics and reassertion of Treasury control over administrative bureaus effectively excluded amateur social scientists from the policy process and altered the relation of science and the state'. Schweber, *Disciplining Statistics*, 12–13. This involved the 'transformation of vital statistics into a form of professional knowledge'.

20 See City League of Help, *Annual Report, 1907–08*, (1908), 15.

21 The interesting case of Alexander McDougall's *Inquiry into the Causes of Pauperism in the Township of Manchester* (1884), initially prompted by Watts, and pursued because the existing statistics lacked the longitudinal data needed to assess causes of pauperism, but which proceeded via visits to selected cases to inquire into their histories. Not just reading houses, but still operating via visiting sampling; but also reporting the results not via specimens, but by a classification of cases.

22 Roger Davidson, 'The State and Social Investigation in Britain, 1880–1914', in Michael J. Lacey and Mary O. Furner, *The State and Social Investigation in Britain and the United States* (1993), 242–75; J. Harris, *Unemployment and Politics: A Study in English Social Policy, 1886–1914* (1972).

23 Roger Davidson, *Whitehall and the Labour Problem in Late Victorian and Edwardian Britain. A Study in Official Statistics and Social Control* (1985).

24 Niven, *Report of the MOH* (1908), 136–40; compare with his investigation of the impact of the occupation of mothers on the health of infants, *Report of the*

MOH (1909), 70–1. For earlier interest, see his exploration of the occupational relations of phthisis, *BMJ* 13 September 1902.

25 For good, e.g. James Niven, 'The Administration of the Manchester Milk Clauses, 1899', *Public Health* (1900–1), 826–35. This is very visible in his MOH reports for the later 1890s, which show much greater attention to the aetiology of disease and an explicit rejection of 'general hygienic improvement' responses to problems of disease, e.g. *Report of the MOH* (1895), 75–84.

26 Anne Hardy, 'Pioneers in the Victorian Provinces: Veterinarians, Public Health and the Urban Animal Economy', *Urban History* 29.3 (2002), 372–87; compare Niven, *Report of Health of City of Manchester* (1902), iv. It is important to recognise that it occurs at around this time, not around 1860, as suggested in Schweber, *Disciplining Statistics*, 112–16.

27 Mooney, *Intrusive Interventions*, 146.

28 Mooney, *Intrusive Interventions*, 161, citing John Robertson, *Special Report on the Prevalence of Tuberculosis and the Measures for its Prevention* (1899), 10.

29 Marr, *Housing Conditions*, 5.

30 The Social Questions Union was established 1892–3, with a focus on social evils such as gambling and prostitution; its conditions of home life committee again sought to exploit the information gathering potential of the Ladies Sanitary Association, see M&SSA *Annual Report* (1894), 7. For the Hulme Healthy Homes Society, see Harold Platt, 'From Hygeia to the Garden City: Bodies, Houses and the Rediscovery of the Slum in Manchester, 1875–1910', *Journal of Urban History* 33.5 (2007), 756–72, and also 'Insanitary Conditions of Hulme', *MWT*, 19 December 1890; *MCN*, 18 November 1893, *MG*, 14 January 1898; for Chorlton, see *MCN*, 13 December 1890, for St Clement's, Ardwick and Longsight Healthy Homes Society, see *MCN*, 26 March 1892. It is notable that this latter society was involved in attempts at 'systematic visitation' so as to be able to report nuisances. For Ancoats, see 'The Rambler in Manchester IX: Helping to Make Healthy Homes in Ancoats', *MCN*, 23 April 1892, 23 September 1893, 27 September 1913. The Social Questions Union had informal links to the Charity Organisation Society, which did not have a local branch in Manchester, see *Charity Organisation Society Review*, n.s. 1 (January–June, 1897), 112.

31 *National Advance*, 3 May 1890, from Hulme Healthy Homes Society 'scrapbooks' in MCL, quoted Platt, 'From Hygeia to the Garden City', 762. Municipal officials shared this emphasis on what Crook describes as 'education via visitation', Crook, *Governing Systems*, 141.

32 See Malcolm Mansfield, 'Putting Moral Standards on the Map: The Construction of Unemployment and the Housing Problem in Turn-of-the-Century London', *Journal of Historical Sociology* 21.2-3 (2008), 166–82. Harold Platt argues that 1889 'became pivotal in moving civic discourse on housing reform from a focus on individual behavior to an emphasis on social environmentalism', Platt, *Shock Cities*, 327.

33 *MOH Report* (1900), 161.

34 Editorials were still talking of dwellings in the later 1890s, see for example *MCN*, 6 March 1897, and it is the Citizen's Committee for the Improvement of Unwholesome Dwellings and Surroundings of the People which prepares Marr's report.

35 For a different mode of discussing Hulme, see, for example, the comments of Rev. J. Lightfoot, *MCN*, 6 February 1904; although even here it is possible to

see an emerging differentiation, with references to a particular block of 'darkest Hulme', *MCN*, 20 February 1904. (In contrast, newspaper reports in the *Manchester Weekly Times* around 1890 do still show a sense of differentiation, even though by then the primary tone was clearly one of monotony.)

36 For example, 'Life in Paradise Court. A City Road Colony and its Inhabitants', *MCN*, 7 February 1891.

37 See Marr, *Housing*, although even here, districts do get some coded identification, as in the 'district in Ancoats, of 12.67 acres, containing nearly 600 dwellings', 54; Mayne, *Imagined Slum*, 130; Ward, *Poverty, Ethnicity, and the American City*.

38 This is visible in the section on 'Manchester and Salford', in *Report of an Enquiry by the Board of Trade into Working Class, Rents, Housing and Retail Prices, Together with Standard Rates of Wages Prevailing in Certain Occupations in the Principal Industrial Towns of the United Kingdom* (1908), 294. Compare the sense in mid-Victorian Manchester that overcrowding was becoming less of an issue, see letter of Royston, *MG*, 1 May 1861.

39 Cited in Marr, *Housing*, 21.

40 Though interestingly the second edition produced in 1893 does try to break down figures to show distinctions of inner and outer districts, and concedes that 'if corresponding facts for the older portions of Manchester were available for contrast with similar facts relating to the newer portions of the City, still more startling differences would be disclosed', Tatham, *Manchester Life Tables* (2nd edn, 1893), v.

41 *MCCP* (1894–5). See, for example, the attempt to control for the age structure of populations and individual households in Niven's Back to Back Houses paper 1895. For university statistics, see Schweber, *Disciplining Statistics*, 188–94.

42 A. Ransome, 'The Need for Combined Medical Observation', *BMJ*, 8 October 1864, *idem*, 'The Scientific and Practical Objects of the Registration of Disease', *BMJ*, 16 September 1882.

43 In which Booth's work series was in some respects transitional, see Rosemary O'Day and David Englander, *Mr Charles Booth's Inquiry. Life and Labour of the People of London Reconsidered* (1993). Hennock, 'Concepts of Poverty', discusses the shift from informant to respondent modes.

44 David Reeder, 'Representations of Metropolis: Descriptions of the Social Environment in Life and Labour', Englander and O'Day, *Retrieved Riches*, 323–38, especially 324.

45 Englander, 'Mayhew and Booth', 132. Booth did not just use SBVs. O'Day and Englander, *Booth Reconsidered*, 8, 18, and *passim*; note a range of interviews, questionnaires, other statistics and other house-to-house visits. Of course, Booth's entire primary plan was spatial, 'to divide the entire population by districts and by groups of trades …. And then deal with each district by a local inquiry', Booth 'The Inhabitants of Tower Hamlets (School Board Division), Their Condition and Occupations', *Journal of the Royal Statistical Society* 50 (1887), 326, cited Topalov, 'City as *terra incognita*', 411. Thomas Gibson-Bryden's recent study balances these earlier approaches by contextualising Booth precisely in the terms suggested by the overall argument here, as 'symptomatic of a larger, morally and religiously inclined culture', *Moral Mapping of Edwardian London*, 42 and *passim*.

46 As in his *Progress of Manchester in the Twenty Years from 1840–1860* (1861), and his *On the Social and Educational Statistics of Manchester and Salford* (1862),

as well as papers such as his study of family expenditure to the British Association at the 1887 Manchester meeting.

47 Farr, *Supplement to the 35th Annual Report of the Registrar General* (1875), iii, quoted in Kerr, *Contagion, Isolation and Biopolitics*, 239.

48 Seth Koven, 'The Dangers of Castle Building', in Bulmer, Bales, Kish Sklar, *Social Survey in Historical Perspective*, 370. For another local instance, see the suggestion of Harold Platt of the Healthy Homes activists of the 1880s and 1890s 'learning door-to-door organizing techniques from trade unionists', Platt, 'From Hygeia to the Garden City', 762.

49 As in Eileen Janes Yeo, 'The Social Survey in Social Perspective, 1830–1930', in Bulmer et al., *Social Survey in Historical Perspective*, 49–65.

50 For Wright and Sims, see Rubenstein, *School Attendance*, 52–3; for Gavin, see Pamela K. Gilbert, 'The Victorian Social Body and Urban Cartography', in Gilbert, *Imagined Londons*, 11–30.

51 See the argument in Mariana Valverde, 'Seeing Like a City: The Dialectic of Modern and Premodern Ways of Seeing in Urban Governance', *Law & Society Review* 45,2 (2011), 277–312.

52 Schweber, *Disciplining Statistics*, 20–2 and *passim*.

53 The concept is from Osborne and Rose, 'Spatial Phenomenotechnics', 210.

54 The work of Otter is exemplary here.

55 This is a line of argument which has affinities with that developed by, for example, Tom Crook in his 'Suspect Figures', 165–84, but also one which attempts to establish a more pervasive counterweight than Carlylean anti-industrialism.

56 As in Frankel, *States of Inquiry*, e.g. 149–52. See Neil Smith and Cindi Katz, 'Grounding Metaphor: Towards a Spatialized Politics', in Michael Keith and Steve Pile, eds, *Place and the Politics of Identity* (1993), 67–83.

57 See, for example, John Pickles, *A History of Spaces: Cartographic Reason, Mapping and the Geo-Coded World* (2004), 12.

58 De Certeau, *The Writing of History*, 126.

Bibliography

Archival sources

Edward Brotherton Scrapbook, M98, Manchester Archives.
Journals of James Bembridge, BR Ms 259.BI, Manchester Archives.
Manchester and Salford Sanitary Association Papers, M126, Manchester Archives.
Manchester Poor Law Union files, Ministry of Health Papers, MH12, National Archives.
Manchester School Board Papers, M65, Manchester Archives.
National Schools Archive, Church of England Record Office.

Parliamentary papers

Poor Law Commissioners Inquiry into the Sanitary State of the Labouring Population of Great Britain (1842).
Report of an Enquiry by the Board of Trade into Working Class, Rents, Housing and Retail Prices, Together with Standard Rates of Wages Prevailing in Certain Occupations in the Principal Industrial Towns of the United Kingdom (1908).
Report of the General Board of Health on the Epidemic Cholera of 1848 and 1849 (1849).
Royal Commission into the Sewage of Towns, Second Report (1861).
Royal Commission on State of Large Towns. First and Second Reports (1844, 1845).
Royal Commission on Vaccination (1897).
Select Committee on Education in Manchester and Salford (1852–3).
Select Committee on Smoke Prevention, Report (1843).
Select Committee on the State of Beerhouses (1869).

Primary printed sources

Joseph Adshead, *Distress in Manchester. Evidence (Tabular and Otherwise) of the State of the Labouring Classes in 1840–42* (1842).
Anon, *Afternoons in the Manchester Slums. By a Lady* (1887).
Anon, *Tales of Manchester Life. By a Manchester Minister* (1870s).

J.A. Bremner, 'By What Means Can the Impediments to the Education of Children of the Manual-Labour Class, Arising from the Apathy or Poverty of Parents, and the Claims of the Market for Labour, Be Most Effectually Removed', *Transactions of the National Association for the Promotion of Social Science* 10 (1866), 307–17.

Edward Brotherton, *Popular Education in Manchester and Salford* (1864).

Edward Brotherton, *Popular Education and Political Economy* (1865).

David Chadwick, *On the Rates of Wages in Manchester and Salford [Paper presented to the London Statistical Society, 1859* (1860).

E.B. Chalmers, *The Parson, the Parish and the Working Man* (1859).

John Chapple and Alan Shelston, eds, *Further Letters of Mrs Gaskell* (2013).

John Chapple and Arthur Pollard, *The Letters of Mrs Gaskell* (1966).

A. Cobden Smith, 'Brooke Herford', *The Sunday School Quarterly* 1 (1909), 118–19.

A. Cobden Smith, 'Mrs Gaskell and Lower Mosley Street', *The Sunday School Quarterly* 3 (January 1911), 156–61.

J.H. Crosfield, *The Bitter Cry of Outcast Ancoats and of Impoverished Manchester* (1887).

Cross Street Chapel, Manchester, *Commemoration of the Fifty Years' Ministry of the Rev. William Gaskell, M.A.* (1878).

George Eliot, 'The Natural History of German Life', *Essays and Leaves from a Notebook* (1884).

Ebenezer Elliott, *The Splendid Village, Corn Law Rhymes and Other Poems*, I (1834).

Elizabeth Gaskell, *Four Short Stories*, introduced by Anna Walters (1993).

Peter Gaskell, *Artisans and Machinery: The Moral and Physical Condition of the Manufacturing Population* (1836).

Henry Gaulter, *The Origin and Progress of the Malignant Cholera in Manchester* (1833).

F.P. Gibbon, 'C.E.B. Russell', in R.S. Forman, ed., *Great Christians* (1933), 483–98.

John Hatton, *A Lecture on the Sanitary Condition of Chorlton upon Medlock* (1854).

Brooke Herford, *Travers Madge: A Memoir* (1867).

Octavia Hill, *District Visiting. A Few Words to Volunteer Visitors Among the Poor* (1876).

Fred Hirst, *The Slums of Manchester* (1888).

'A Manchester Correspondent' [Mat Hompes], 'Mrs. Gaskell and Her Social Work Among the Poor', *The Inquirer and Christian Life* (London) (8 October 1910).

Margaret Howitt, *Mary Howitt, Her Autobiography* (1889).

Alexander Ireland, ed., *Selections from the Letters of Geraldine Endsor Jewsbury to Jane Welsh Carlyle* (1892).

Geraldine Jewsbury, *Marian Withers* (1851).

Joseph Johnson, *Heroines of Our Times. Sketches* (1860).

James Kay-Shuttleworth, *The Moral and Physical Condition of the Working Classes Employed in the Cotton Manufacture in Manchester* (1832).

James Kay-Shuttleworth, *Four Periods of Public Education as Reviewed in 1832–1839–1846–1862* (1862).

W.J. Kennedy, 'On the Principles to be Observed in Schemes Promoting School Attendance', in A Hill, ed., *Essays Upon Educational Subjects* (1857), 226–39.

John Leigh, *Report on Infectious Diseases in Manchester* (1871).

William Logan, *The Great Social Evil: Its Causes, Extent, Results and Remedies* (1871).

C.F. Lowder, *Ten Years in S. George's Mission. Being an Account of Its Origins, Progress and Works of Mercy* (1867).

J.W. MacGill, *Manchester at Night. Its Sins and Sufferings* (1886).

Manchester City Council, *Proceedings of the City Council* (1838–1914).

Manchester City Mission, *Annual Reports* (1838–1873).

Manchester Statistical Society, *Report of a Committee of the Manchester Statistical Society on the Condition of the Working Classes in an Extensive Manufacturing District in 1834, 1835 and 1836* (1838).

T.R. Marr, *Housing Conditions in Manchester and Salford* (1904).

Alexander McDougall, *Drink and Poverty* (1891).

J.E. Mercer, *The Conditions of Life in Angel Meadow* (1897).

National Education League, *Report of the First Meeting of Members of the National Education League* (1869).

W.B. Neale, *Juvenile Delinquency in Manchester: Its Causes and History* (1840).

James Niven, 'The Administration of the Manchester Milk Clauses, 1899', *Public Health* 13 (1900–1), 826–35.

E.J. Nixon, *A Manual of District Visiting* (1848).

Daniel Noble, *The Influence of Manufacturers on Health and Life* (1843).

Joseph Nunn, *Strictures on the Reports on Education in Manchester, Liverpool, Birmingham and Leeds, presented to the House of Commons by Messrs J.G. Fitch and D.R. Fearon etc ... addressed to the Rt Hon W.E. Forster* (1870).

Henry C. Oats, 'Inquiry into the Educational and Other Conditions of a District in Deansgate', *Transactions of the Manchester Statistical Society* 11 (1864–5), 1–13.

Arthur Ransome, 'On the Need for a Systematic Study of Epidemic Disease', *BMJ* 2 (27 August 1881), 353–54.

Arthur Ransome, 'Where Consumption is Bred in Manchester and Salford', *Health Journal* 5 (November 1887), 88–90.

Arthur Ransome, 'On the need of Combined Medical Observation', *BMJ* 2 (8 October 1864), 405–6.

Arthur Ransome and William Royston, *Report Upon the Health of Manchester and Salford* (1867).

Arthur Ransome and William Royston, 'The Scientific and Practical Objects of the Registration of Disease', *BMJ* 2 (16 September 1882), 505–7.

[Angus Reach] C. Aspin, ed., *Manchester and the Textile Districts in 1849* (1972).

Charles Richson, *Education in Manchester. Considered with Special Reference to the State of Church Day Schools and the Means of Extending Education Generally* (1850).

Charles Richson, *A Sketch of Some of the Causes which, in Manchester, Induced the Abandonment of the Voluntary System in Support of Schools, and the Introduction of the Manchester and Salford Education Bill* (1851).

Charles Richson, *Educational Facts and Statistics of Manchester* (1852).

Charles Richson, 'On the Importance of Statistical and Economical Inquiries', *Transactions of the Manchester Statistical Society* (1857–8).

Margaret Shaen, *Memorials of Two Sisters: Susanna and Catherine Winkworth* (1908).

John Tatham, *Manchester Life Tables* (2nd edn, 1893).

John C. Thresh, *An Enquiry into the Causes of the Excessive Mortality in No. 1 District, Ancoats* (1889).

Walter Tomlinson, *Bye-Ways of Manchester Life* (1887).

Andrew Ure, *The Philosophy of Manufactures: or, an Exposition of the Scientific, Moral and Commercial Economy of the Factory System of Great Britain* (London, 1835).

John Watts, *Report of a Statistical Enquiry of the Executive Committee of the N.P.S.A. in St. Michael's and St. John's Wards*; Manchester. *November and December 1852* (Manchester, 1853).

John Watts, *Work of the First Manchester School Board* (1873).

John Watts, 'Fifteen Years of School Board Work in Manchester', *Transactions of the Manchester Statistical Society* 32 (1885–6), 80–116.

J. Whitehead, *The Rate of Mortality in Manchester* (1863).

T.R. Wilkinson, 'Report on the Educational and Other Conditions of a District at Gaythorn and Knott Mill, Manchester, Visited in January 1868, with Observations Suggested by the Visitation', *Transactions of the Manchester Statistical Society* 14 (1867–8), 53–77.

Secondary sources

T.S. Ashton, *Economic and Social Investigation in Manchester, 1833–1933* (1934).

Carolyn Vellenga Berman, '"Awful Unknown Quantities": Addressing the Readers in *Hard Times*', *Victorian Literature and Culture* 37.2 (September 2009), 561–82.

Karen Boiko, 'Reading and (Re)Writing Class: Elizabeth Gaskell's *Wives and Daughters*', *Victorian Literature and Culture* 33.1 (2005), 85–106.

Lucy E. Bosworth, 'Home Missionaries to the Poor: Abraham Hume and Spiritual Destitution in Liverpool, 1847–1884', *Transactions of the Lancashire and Cheshire Antiquarian Society* 143 (1993), 57–83.

M. Bulmer, ed., *Essays on the History of British Sociological Research* (1985).

Mervyn Busteed, 'Little Islands of Erin: Irish Settlement and Identity in Mid-Nineteenth Century Manchester', in Donald M. MacRaild, ed., *The Great Famine and Beyond: Irish Migrants in Britain in the Nineteenth and Twentieth Centuries* (2000), 94–127.

Alison Byerly, '"A Prodigious Map Beneath His Feet": Virtual Travel and The Panoramic Perspective', *Nineteenth-Century Contexts* 29.2 (2007), 151–68.

Deborah Carlin, '"What Methods Have Brought Blessing": Discourses of Reform in Philanthropic Literature', in Joyce Warner, ed., *The (Other) American Traditions* (1993), 203–25.

Tina Young Choi, *Anonymous Connections: The Body and Narratives of the Social in Victorian Britain* (2016).

David Churchill, *Crime Control and Everyday Life in the Victorian City* (2018).

Danielle Coriale, 'Gaskell's Naturalist', *Nineteenth-Century Literature* 63.3 (2008), 346–75.

Denis Cosgrove, *Geography & Vision: Seeing, Imagining and Representing the World* (2008).

Eleanor Courtemanche, *The 'Invisible Hand' and British Fiction, 1818–1860* (2011).

Tom Crook, 'Secrecy and Liberal Modernity in Victorian and Edwardian England', in Simon Gunn and James Vernon, eds, *The Peculiarities of Liberal Modernity in Imperial Britain* (2011), 72–90.

Tom Crook, 'Suspect Figures. Statistics and Public Trust in Victorian England', in Cook and O'Hara, eds, *Statistics and the Public Sphere* (2011).

Tom Crook, *Governing Systems: Modernity and the Making of Public Health in England, 1830–1910* (2016).

Tom Crook and Glen O'Hara, eds, *Statistics and the Public Sphere: Numbers and the People in Modern Britain, 1800–2000* (2011).

Michael J. Cullen, *The Statistical Movement in Early Victorian Britain. The Foundations of Empirical Social Research* (1975).

Roger Davidson, *Whitehall and the Labour Problem in Late Victorian and Edwardian Britain. A Study in Official Statistics and Social Control* (1985).

Roger Davidson, 'The State and Social Investigation in Britain, 1880–1914', in Michael J. Lacey and Mary O. Furner, eds, *The State and Social Investigation in Britain and the United States* (1993), 242–75.

Celia Davies, 'The Health Visitor as Mother's Friend: A Woman's Place in Public Health, 1900–14', *Social History of Medicine* 1.1 (1988), 39–59.

Andrew Davies, 'Youth Gangs, Masculinity and Violence in late Victorian Manchester and Salford', *Journal of Social History* 32.2 (1998), 349–69.

Andrew Davies, '"These Viragoes are No Less Cruel than the Lads": Young Women, Gangs and Violence in Late Victorian Manchester and Salford', *British Journal of Criminology* 39.1 (1999), 72–89.

Anna Davin, *Growing Up Poor: School and Street in London, 1870–1914* (1996).

Michel de Certeau, *The Practices of Everyday Life*, Volume 1 (1984).

Sandra M. Den Otter, *British Idealism and Social Explanation* (1996).

Richard Dennis, *Cities in Modernity* (2008).

Alain Desrosieres, *The Politics of Large Numbers. A History of Statistical Reasoning* (1998).

Robert Dowling, *Slumming in New York: From the Waterfront to Mythic Harlem* (2007).

Barry M. Doyle, 'Mapping Slums in a Historic City: Representing Working Class Communities in Edwardian Norwich', *Planning Perspectives* 16 (2001), 47–65.

Felix Driver, *Geography Militant. Cultures of Exploration and Empire* (2001).

Felix Driver, 'Moral Geographies: Social Science and the Urban Environment in Mid-Nineteenth Century England', *Transactions of the Institute of British Geographers*, NS, 13 (1988), 275–87.

Angus Easson, *Elizabeth Gaskell* (1979).

David Elesh, 'The Manchester Statistical Society: A Case Study of Discontinuity in the History of Empirical Social Research', in A. Oberschall, ed., *The Establishment of Empirical Sociology: Studies in Continuity, Discontinuity and Institutionalization* (1972).

Dorice Williams Elliott, 'The Female Visitor and the Marriage of Classes in Gaskell's *North and South*', *Nineteenth Century Literature* 49 (1994), 21–49.

Jim Endersby, *Imperial Science. Joseph Hooker and the Practices of Victorian Science* (2008).

David Englander, *Landlord and Tenant in Urban Britain, 1838–1918* (1983).

David Englander and Rosemary O'Day, *Retrieved Riches. Social Investigation in Britain, 1840–1914* (1995).

Jonathan V. Farina, '"A Certain Shadow": Personified Abstractions and the Form of *Household Words*', *Victorian Periodicals Review* 42 (2009), 392–415.

Robert Fishman, *Bourgeois Utopias: The Rise and Fall of Suburbia* (1987).

Robert Fishman, *East End 1888: A Year in a London Borough Among the Labouring Poor* (1988).

Oz Frankel, *States of Inquiry: Social Investigations and Print Culture in Nineteenth-Century Britain and the United States* (2006).

Monica Correa Fryckstedt, '*Mary Barton* and the *Reports of the Ministry to the Poor*: A New Source', *Studia Neophilologica* 50 (1980), 333–6.

Matthew Gandy, 'The Bacteriological City and its Discontents', *Historical Geography* 34 (2006), 14–25.

Catherine Gallagher, *The Body Economic* (2005).

Thomas R.C. Gibson-Bryden, *Moral Mapping of Edwardian London. Charles Booth, Christian Charity and the Poor-but-Respectable* (2018).

Pamela K. Gilbert, '"Scarcely to Be Described": Urban Extremes as Real Spaces and Mythic Places in the London Cholera Epidemic of 1854', *Nineteenth Century Studies* 14 (2000), 149–72.

Pamela K. Gilbert, ed., *Imagined Londons* (2002).

Pamela K. Gilbert, *Mapping the Victorian Social Body* (2004).

Pamela K. Gilbert, *The Citizen's Body. Desire, Health and the Social in Victorian England* (2007).

Pamela K. Gilbert, *Cholera and Nation: Doctoring the Social Body in Victorian England* (2008).

Lawrence Goldman, *Science, Reform and Politics in Victorian Britain* (2002).

Lauren Goodlad, *Victorian Literature and the Victorian State. Character and Governance in a Liberal Society* (2003).

Robert Gray, *The Factory Question and Industrial England* (1996).

John Gross, 'Mrs Gaskell', in Ian Watt, ed., *The Victorian Novel. Modern Essays in Criticism* (1971), 217–28.

Simon Gunn, 'From Hegemony to Governmentality: Changing Perceptions of Power in Social History', *Journal of Social History* 31.2 (2006), 705–20.

Matthew G. Hannah, *Governmentality and the Mastery of Territory in Nineteenth-Century America* (2000).

Anne Hardy, 'Pioneers in the Victorian Provinces: Veterinarians, Public Health and the Urban Animal Economy', *Urban History* 29.3 (2002), 372–87.

J.B. Harley, 'Maps, Knowledge and Power', in Denis Cosgrove and Stephen Daniels, eds, *The Iconography of Landscape* (1988), 277–12.

Nick Hayes, '"Calculating Class": Housing, Lifestyle and Status in the Provincial English City, 1900–1950', *Urban History* 36.1 (2009), 113–40.

E.P. Hennock, 'Concepts of Poverty in British Social Surveys from Charles Booth to Arthur Bowley', in M. Bulmer, ed., *The Social Survey in Historical Perspective* (1991).

Martin Hewitt, 'The Travails of District Visiting: Manchester 1830–1870', *Historical Research* 71 (1998), 196–227.

Martin Hewitt, 'Fifty Years Ahead of Its Time? The Provident Dispensaries Movement in Manchester, 1871–1885', in Alan Kidd and Melanie Tebbutt, eds, *Essays in Honour of Mike Rose* (2017), 84–108.

Anne Humpherys, *Travels into the Poor Man's Country. The Work of Henry Mayhew* (1977).

Katherine Inglis, 'Unimagined Community and Disease in *Ruth*', in Lesa Scholl and Emily Morris, eds, *Place and Progress in the Works of Elizabeth Gaskell* (2015), 67–82.

H.C. Irvine, *The Old D.P.S.* (1933).

Audrey Jaffe, *The Affective Life of the Average Man. The Victorian Novel and the Stock Market Graph* (2010).

Frederic Jameson, *The Political Unconscious. Narrative as Socially Symbolic Act* (1981).

Karen Jones and K. Williamson, 'The Birth of the Schoolroom', *Ideology and Consciousness* 6 (1979), 59–110.

Patrick Joyce, *The Rule of Freedom: Liberalism and the Modern City* (2003).

Robert H. Kargon, *Science in Victorian Manchester* (1977).

John R. Kellet, *The Impact of Railways on the Victorian City* (1969).

Edith Kelly and Thomas Kelly, eds, *A Schoolmaster's Notebook* (1957).

Matthew L. Newsom Kerr, *Contagion, Isolation, and Biopolitics in Victorian London* (2018).

Amy King, 'Taxonomical Cures: The Politics of Natural History and Herbalist Medicine in Elizabeth Gaskell's Mary Barton', in Noah Heringman, ed., *Romantic Science: The Literary Forms of Natural History* (2003), 255–70.

Michael Klotz, 'Manufacturing Fictional Individuals: Victorian Social Statistics, the Novel, and Great Expectations', *Novel* 46.2 (2013), 214–33.

Seth Koven, *Slumming. Sexual and Social Politics in Victorian London* (2004).

Carolyn Lambert, *The Meanings of Home in Elizabeth Gaskell's Fiction* (2013).

Caroline Levine, 'The Enormity Effect: Realist Fiction, Literary Studies and the Refusal to Count', *Genre* 50.1 (April 2017), 61–75.

Kathrin Levitan, *A Cultural History of the British Census: Envisioning the Multitude in the Nineteenth Century* (2011).

Ruth Livesey, 'Women Rent Collectors and the Rewriting of Space, Class and Gender in East London, 1870–1900', in Elizabeth Darling, Lesley Whitworth, eds, *Women and the Making of Built Space in England, 1870–1950* (2007), 87–105.

György Lukács, *Studies in European Realism* (2002).

Bill Luckin, 'Revisiting the Slums in Manchester and Salford in the 1930s', in B. Doyle, ed., *Urban Politics and Space in the Nineteenth and Twentieth Centuries: Regional Perspectives* (2007), 134–47.

Gage McWeeny, 'The Sociology of the Novel: George Eliot's Strangers', *Novel* 42.3 (2009), 538–45.

Gage McWeeny, *The Comfort of Strangers: Social Life and Literary Form* (2016).

S.E. Maltby, *Manchester and the Movement for National Elementary Education, 1800–1870* (1918).

Malcolm Mansfield, 'Putting Moral Standards on the Map: The Construction of Unemployment and the Housing Problem in Turn-of-the-Century London', *Journal of Historical Sociology* 21.2–3 (2008), 166–82.

David Matless, 'Regional Surveys and Local Knowledges: The Geographical Imagination in Britain, 1918–39' *Transactions of the Institute of British Geographers*, NS 17 (1992), 464–80.

Alan Mayne, *The Imagined Slum: Newspaper Representation in Three Cities, 1870–1914* (1983).

Graham Mooney, *Intrusive Interventions: Public Health, Domestic Space, and Infectious Disease Surveillance in England, 1840–1914* (2015).

Lyn Nead, 'From Alleys to Courts: Obscenity and the Mapping of Mid-Victorian London', *New Formations* 37 (Spring 1999), 33–46.

Lyn Nead, *Victorian Babylon. People, Streets and Images in Nineteenth Century London* (2000).

Marjaana Niemi, 'Public Health Discourses in Birmingham and Gothenburg, 1890–1920', in S. Sheard and H. Power, eds, *Body and City: Histories of Urban Public Health* (2000), 123–42.

Deborah Epstein Nord, *Walking the Victorian Streets. Women, Representation and the City* (1995).

Rosemary O'Day and David Englander, *Mr Charles Booth's Inquiry. Life and Labour of the People of London Reconsidered* (1993).

Thomas Osborne and Nikolas Rose, 'Governing Cities: Notes on the Spatialisation of Virtue', *Environment and Planning D: Society and Space* 17 (1999), 737–60.

Thomas Osborne and Nikolas Rose, 'Spatial Phenomenotechnics: Making Space with Charles Booth and Patrick Geddes', *Environment and Planning D: Society and Space* 22 (2004), 209–28.

Chris Otter, *The Victorian Eye, A Political History of Light in Britain, 1800–1910* (2008).

Dean Pavlakis, 'Reputation and the Sexual Abuse of Boys: Changing Norms in Late-Nineteenth-Century Britain', *Men and Masculinities* 17.3 (2014), 231–52.

W.S.F. Pickering, 'Abraham Hume (1814–1884): A Forgotten Pioneer of Religious Sociology', *Archives de Sociologie des Religions* 33 (January–June 1972), 33–48.

John Pickles, *A History of Spaces: Cartographic Reason, Mapping and the Geo-Coded World* (2004).

John V. Pickstone, 'Dearth, Dirt and Fever Epidemics: Rewriting the History of British "Public Health", 1750–1850', in Terence Ranger, ed., *Epidemics and Ideas: Essays on the Historical Perception of Pestilence* (1992), 125–48.

John V. Pickstone, 'Ways of Knowing: Toward a Historical Sociology of Science, Technology and Medicine', *British Journal for the History of Science* 26 (December 1993), 433–58.

Harold L. Platt, *Shock Cities: The Environmental Transformation and Reform of Manchester and Chicago* (2005).

Harold L. Platt, 'From Hygeia to the Garden City: Bodies, Houses and the Rediscovery of the Slum in Manchester, 1875–1910', *Journal of Urban History* 33.5 (2007), 756–72.

Mary Poovey, *Making a Social Body: British Cultural Formation, 1830–1864* (1995).

Mary Poovey, *A History of the Modern Fact. Problems of Knowledge in the Sciences of Wealth and Society* (1998).

Frank K. Prochaska, *Women and Philanthropy in Nineteenth Century England* (1980).

Paul Rabinow, *French Modern: Norms and Forms of the Social Environment* (1989).

John Rex, *Race, Community and Conflict* (1967).

Henry Roper, 'Toward an Elementary Education Act for England and Wales, 1865–68', *British Journal of Educational Studies* 23 (1975), 181–208.

Brian Rosa, 'Beneath the Arches: Re-appropriating the Spaces of Infrastructure in Manchester', unpublished PhD, University of Manchester (2014).

Michael E. Rose, 'Settlement of University Men in Great Towns: University Settlements in Manchester and Liverpool', *Transactions of the Historic Society of Lancashire and Cheshire* 139 (1990), 137–60.

Michael E. Rose, 'The Manchester University Settlement in Ancoats, 1895–1909', *Manchester Region History Review* 7 (1993), 55–62.

Ellen Ross, *Slum Travellers: Ladies and London Poverty, 1860–1920* (2007).

David Rubinstein, *School Attendance in London, 1870–1914: A Social History* (1969).

Hilary Schor, *Scheherazade in the Marketplace. Elizabeth Gaskell and the Victorian Novel* (1992).

Libby Schweber, *Disciplining Statistics: Demography and Vital Statistics in France and England, 1830–1885* (2006).

James C. Scott, *Seeing Like a State* (1998).

Anne Secord, 'Elizabeth Gaskell and the Artisan Naturalists of Manchester', *Gaskell Society Journal* 19 (2005), 34–51.

John Seed, 'Unitarianism, Political Economy and the Antinomies of Liberal Culture in Manchester, 1830–50', *Social History* 7 (1982), 1–25.

William Sharpe and Leonard Wallock, 'From "Great Town" to "Nonplace urban realm": Reading the Modern City', in Sharpe and Wallock, eds, *Visions of the Modern City: Essays in History, Art and Literature* (1987), 1–50.

John Geoffrey Sharps, *Mrs Gaskell's Observation and Invention: A Study of Her Non-Biographic Works* (1970).

Alan Shelston, '*Ruth*: Mrs Gaskell's Neglected Novel', *Bulletin of the John Rylands Library* 58.1 (1975), 173–92.

Daniel Siegel, *Charity and Condescension: Victorian Literature and the Dilemmas of Philanthropy* (2012).

Emily Steinlight, *Populating the Novel. Literary Form and the Politics of Surplus Life* (2018).

Patsy Stoneman, *Elizabeth Gaskell* (2006).

Becky Taylor and Ben Rogaly, '"Mrs Fairly is a Dirty, Lazy Type": Unsatisfactory Households and the Problem of Problem Families, Norwich 1942 to 1963', *Twentieth Century British History* 18 (2007), 429–52.

Arnold Thackray, 'Natural Knowledge in Cultural Context: The Manchester Model', *American Historical Review* 79.3 (1974), 672–709.

Beth Fowkes Tobin, *Superintending the Poor. Charitable Ladies and Paternal Landlords in British Fiction, 1770–1860* (1993).

Christian Topalov, 'The City as Terra Incognita: Charles Booth's Poverty Survey and the People of London, 1886–1891', *Planning Perspectives* 8 (1993), 395–425.

Alison Twells, *The Civilising Mission and the English Middle Class, 1792–1850: The 'Heathen' at Home and Overseas* (2008).

Jenny Uglow, *Elizabeth Gaskell. A Habit of Stories* (1993).

Marianne Valverde, 'The Dialectic of the Familiar and the Unfamiliar: The "Jungle" in Early Slum Travel Writing', *Sociology* 30 (1996), 493–509.

Gregory Vargo, 'Questions from Workers Who Read; Education and Self-Formation in Chartist Print Culture and Elizabeth Gaskell's *Mary Barton*', in his *An Underground History of Early Victorian Fiction. Chartism, Radical Print Culture, and the Social Problem Novel* (2018), 115–47.

Laura Vaughan, 'Jewish Immigrant Settlement Patterns in Manchester and Leeds 1881', *Urban Studies* 43.3 (2006), 653–72.

Judith R. Walkowitz, *City of Dreadful Delight. Narratives of Sexual Danger in Late Victorian London* (1992).

Ross Douglas Waller, *Letters Addressed to Mrs Gaskell by Celebrated Contemporaries* (1935).

David Ward, *Poverty, Ethnicity, and the American City, 1840–1925: Changing Conceptions of the Slum and the Ghetto* (1989).

Bill Williams, *The Making of Manchester Jewry, 1740–1875* (1985).

David A.P. Womble, 'Phineas Finn, the Statistics of Character, and the Sensorium of Liberal Personhood', *Novel* 51.1 (2018), 17–35.

Edgar Wright, *Mrs Gaskell. The Basis for Reassessment* (1965).

Terry Wyke and Alan Kidd, *The Challenge of Cholera: Proceedings of the Manchester Special Board of Health 1831–1833* (2010).

Terry Wyke, Brian Robson, Martin Dodge, *Manchester: Mapping the City* (2018).

J.A. Yelling, *Slums and Slum Clearance in Victorian London* (1986).

Eileen Yeo, *The Contest for Social Science. Relations and Representations of Gender and Class* (1996).

Eileen Yeo, 'Social Surveys in the 18th and 19th Centuries', in Theodore Porter and Dorothy Ross, eds, *Cambridge History of Science, Vol. 7: The Modern Social Sciences* (2003).

A.F. Young and E.T. Ashton, *British Social Work in the Nineteenth Century* (1956).

Index